Other books by Thomas H. Green, S.J.

OPENING TO GOD
WHEN THE WELL RUNS DRY
DARKNESS IN THE MARKETPLACE

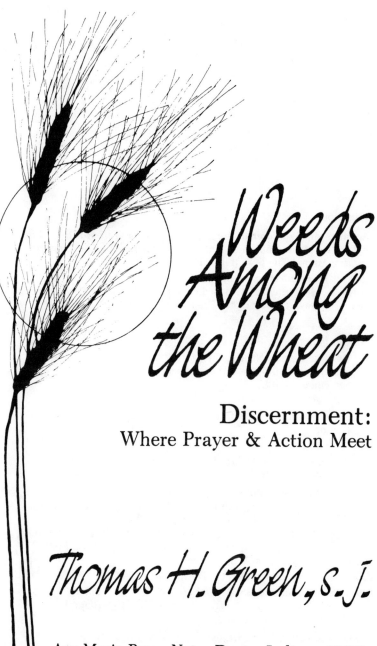

Weeds Among the Wheat

Discernment:
Where Prayer & Action Meet

Thomas H. Green, S.J.

Ave Maria Press, Notre Dame, Indiana 46556

Permissions

Excerpts from *Wayfarer in the Land* by Hannah Hurnard. Published by Tyndale House Publishers, Inc. with permission of The Church's Ministry Among The Jews (Olive Press).

Excerpts from *Discernment of Spirits* by Jacques Guillet. Copyright © 1970 by The Order of St. Benedict, Inc. Published by The Liturgical Press, Collegeville, Minnesota. Used with permission.

Imprimi Potest:

Rev. Bienvenido Nebres, S.J.
Provincial, Philippine Province Society of Jesus
September 8, 1983

Nihil Obstat:

Msgr. Josephino S. Ramirez
Censor

Imprimatur:

+ Jaime Cardinal L. Sin, D.D.
Archbishop of Manila

Library of Congress Catalog Card Number: 84-70663
International Standard Book Number: 0-87793-319-7 (Cloth)
0-87793-318-9 (Paper)

Cover design: Thomas Ringenberg
Printed and bound in the United States of America.

Contents

Preface

The past, even when it is shaped by the "accidents of God," sets the pattern of our expectations for the future. When I returned to Rochester, New York, in April of 1983, most of my friends assumed — correctly — that I must be planning to write another book. The usual question was, "Is it to be a sequel to the other three? A further development of the prayer theme?" I generally replied that this time I had a new topic, related to prayer but not really a sequel to the earlier books. This time the subject was to be discernment, the meeting point of prayer and action in the life of the Christian apostle. Now that people had become used to the strange phenomenon of a Jesuit writing about John of the Cross and Teresa of Avila, I was going to surprise them by writing a thoroughly "Jesuit" book, one that drew almost entirely on the teaching of the founder of the Society of Jesus, St. Ignatius Loyola.

While I have found it dangerous to predict too confidently how my books will turn out, in this case the result has been very close to my expectations. Although chapters 8 and 9 do reveal more continuity than anticipated between this book and the first two (*Opening to God* and *When the Well Runs Dry*) and while, as I hope to show in the Introduction, I saw *Darkness in the Marketplace* in a new light after completing the present manuscript, still this book has been, in the writing, the least surprising for me. No "Marthas" have appeared unexpectedly, from between the lines of the outline, to assert their influence on the unfolding argument. This itself was the surprise, since I had come to expect the unexpected!

Nonetheless, it is a joy to have written, as expected and as I hope, a completely "Jesuit" book. St. Ignatius is my own father in the Lord — as close to my heart, I like to believe, as he was to the

7

heart of St. Francis Xavier. Of the two first Jesuit saints, Xavier is the much more romantic figure; I identified much more readily with him in my early years as a Jesuit. But gradually I came to realize why Xavier himself, in India, knelt (and wept) when he read letters from Ignatius in Rome. Xavier knew in his heart what Vatican II was to affirm 400 years later: that the charism of the founder is the lifeblood of a religious congregation, continuing to flow in its members for as long as it survives. Ignatius was the "father of his soul," and gradually I came to realize how profoundly true this is for me also.

We are human, of course. And for this reason Ignatius must be reincarnated for us Jesuits in the people we know and love today. I suppose each of us has his or her own experiences of reincarnation. For myself, I think of Father Leonard Boase, S.J., who died in the early months of 1983 as I was beginning work on this book. His classic *Prayer of Faith*, as I have said elsewhere, played a crucial role in my own discovery of the true meaning of contemplation in action. While I never met him, he surely was instrumental in making Ignatius live for me today. I also recall another great Jesuit, whom I did meet: Father Pedro Arrupe, the recently retired Superior General of the Society of Jesus. He was the first Basque General since St. Ignatius himself, and I know I speak for all my Jesuit confreres in saying that he made Ignatius live in our times. Notwithstanding all the difficulty and confusion of this age of *aggiornamento*, it has been a joy to belong to a family gifted with a father—buoyant, strong, faith-filled, loving, exuberant—like Father Arrupe.

Despite their great influence on my life, however, Father Boase and Father Arrupe were still somewhat distant figures. They incarnated Ignatius, but in turn they needed to be incarnated, for me, in the Jesuits whom I knew in the flesh, elbow-to-elbow. There have been many such, of course, but I would like to dedicate this book especially to four of them. During my recent stay in the U.S. I had occasion to see each of the four again, after several years apart. We were all seminarians together and we have since gone our separate apostolic ways. We belong to the transitional generation, formed before Vatican II and called to live in an entirely different, post-Vatican II world. Ours was the time of huge numbers of vocations (there were 130 in our novitiate) and of the greatest losses of vocations in the post-conciliar turmoil. As I visited again with my four old friends—Fathers Tom Wheeler of Washington, D.C., Tom McManus of New York City, and Ernie Sweeney and Herb Ryan of Los Angeles—and realized that all of them had adjusted, happily though not without pain, to the new world in which we live, I saw all my own hopes and struggles mirrored in them. And I realized for the first time what a miracle it is to have survived and grown in "this least Society," to which Ignatius gave all the best of himself.

When we were young seminarians, we used to find it strange and funny that the old, infirm fathers and brothers with whom we lived would ask us to "pray for my perseverance in the Society." At their age and in their condition, we used to wonder, why would they even doubt their perseverance? If they ever left the Jesuits now, where would they go? The very possibility conjured up bizarre images for us! Now, however, we are older and wiser, and the old men's plea seems far from foolish. Perseverance "until the end" is indeed the greatest of God's gifts to any human being, whether it be in the faith commitment of marriage or in that of celibacy. And even though Tom Wheeler, Tom McManus, Ernie, Herb and I are still perhaps some distance from the "end," our perseverance for these almost 35 years of change and challenge seems grace enough.

As always, many people have shared in the writing of this book. In addition to those whom I acknowledged in the earlier books and who have been just as much a part of this one, I should like to thank my cousins, Rie and Skip Rague. They provided me with the services of an excellent typist, Mrs. Julie Christel. (Rie, by the way, is the cousin who reads cookbooks for entertainment, as I read maps!) Also Father Jim Callan, the charismatic pastor of the inner-city parish, Corpus Christi in Rochester, who welcomed me into his remarkable and variegated parish family, and who shared with me Marie van Huben and Mary and Fred Locke and Sylvia Kostin, all of whom helped in the writing and typing of the manuscript. They, and many other parishioners, were also the willing guinea pigs for the testing of the ideas in this book.

In the end, though, it seems most appropriate to dedicate this work on discernment to my four friends and companions on the journey of the past 35 years: Herb Ryan, Ernie Sweeney, Tom McManus and Tom Wheeler. Our perseverance in the Society of Jesus is, above all, a schooling in that discerning love of which we shall speak. It is, for me, a tangible celebration of the spirit of Leonard Boase and Pedro Arrupe which, when all is said and done, is but the living spirit of our father in the Lord, St. Ignatius himself. May they (and all my friends) find much of themselves and of our journey in these pages.

January 1, 1984
Titular Feast of The Society of Jesus

Introduction:
The Meeting Point of Prayer and Action

More than at any other time in the history of the church, we men and women of today live in an age of discernment. The word, that is, is common coinage in contemporary religious circles. Individual religious and religious communities are called to discern the Lord's will for them in the concrete circumstances of their lives. Charismatic communities discern the source and meaning of the prophetic words spoken in their prayer meetings. Young people discern their vocations, and their elders discern the meaning of the challenges and opportunities which arise in the living of their chosen vocations. And spiritual directors are now co-discerners — no longer, as in a simpler, earlier age, called merely to declare God's will to their directees, but now asked to be interpreters who guide others to a mature understanding of the call of the Spirit speaking within them.

When we speak of discernment in all these diverse contexts, we have some vague sense of what we mean by it. We know that the new stress on subsidiarity and collegiality in the post-Vatican II church has called *every* Christian to a responsible, prophetic role in living and proclaiming the faith. And we realize that this implies a more participative, less authoritarian approach to discovering the will of God. Each of us must be in touch with the Spirit of God at work in us. We cannot simply follow the leader and expect the will of God to come to us ready-made from on high. Indeed, authority still has its rightful place in the divine scheme; but, as we noted in chapter 3 of *Opening to God*, authority can no longer (and really never could) dot all the "i"s and cross all the "t"s in the Lord's plan for our lives. It can, and must, give us the general guidelines for our life in Christ. Within this general framework, however, each of us has a unique personal vocation to live. No two of us hear exactly the same call from the Lord; no two of us live exactly the same life.

11

This much is clear to reflective men and women of the church today. It is an exhilarating challenge, one of the most exciting and promising aspects of Christian life in the late 20th century. But it does pose a problem. In a real sense, it was easier to live in an earlier age when God's will was (or seemed to be) clearly and precisely manifested in the commands of ecclesiastical superiors. We may have chafed under the constraints of the old code of canon law and the old autocratic style of government of pastors and bishops, but at least we knew exactly how much meat on Friday constituted a mortal sin and when a missed Mass was grave matter for confession. We had the security of the child, paid for with the coin of perpetual religious adolescence. Now we are called to mature, responsible obedience to God. And the cost of maturing—the obscurity, the personal responsibility for our choices, the need to *know* God and understand his ways for ourselves—is often alarming. Perhaps we realize that Paul's words, immediately after he describes the "spiritual man" as one able to "appraise everything, though he himself can be appraised by no one," are really addressed to us: "Brothers, the trouble was that I could not talk to you as spiritual men but only as men of flesh, as infants in Christ. I fed you with milk, and did not give you solid food, because you were not ready for it. You are not ready for it even now" (1 Cor 3:1-2).

Are we ready for the solid food of mature men and women in Christ? Many, perhaps, are still infants in the Lord; and some even retreat to the womb when they find the real world too threatening. But I am convinced that there are also many, some of whom I have had the joy to direct, ready and willing to mature in Christ Jesus. Their problem, as with the first disciples, is that they need Someone to guide them. They need to learn how to *discern*, how to take responsibility for their own lives and how to read the face of God.

By the grace of this good God, there is much being written today on the art of discernment, and much of it of excellent quality.[1] The only problem, as I see it, is that most of the treatments

---

1 For some of the sources which I have found most helpful, see the references cited below in chapter 1, footnote 1; chapter 5, footnote 2; and the Epilogue, footnote 2. In each case, the authors cited also give extensive bibliographical references.

thus far have been rather specialized and technical.

Thus they might be too heavy for the average "lay" (i.e., not professionally trained in theology or spirituality) Christian pray-er. Hence the challenge and the purpose of this book: to translate into the language of the educated, committed layperson (whether priest or religious or lay) the basic meaning and principles on the art of Christian discernment. It is the same challenge I have faced, for the past several years, in teaching a course on discern-ment in the pastoral theology program of the Loyola School of Theology.

The structure of this book is essentially the structure of that course. I have even incorporated the device of proposing a "prac-ticum question" at the end of each chapter. The students have found these questions, which are intended to apply the content of the lectures and the basic principles of discernment to their own life-experience, one of the most helpful parts of the whole course. During the week between lectures they attempt to formulate their own solutions to the questions proposed. Then in the first hour of the next class, they meet together in small groups of seven or eight to share their solutions and to discuss any obscure points. I then collect their written answers, to read and comment upon them in some detail during the following week. I also give my own "solu-tion" to the problems proposed at the beginning of the lecture ses-sion which follows the small group discussion. For those of you who are reading the book with a group, it might be possible — and very fruitful — to follow the same general format. But even the solitary reader will, I trust, find it helpful to use the practicum questions at the end of each chapter (to which my own answers are given in the Epilogue) as a test of understanding and a prac-tical application of what has been read. Discernment, like prayer, is an art: that is, it is learned by doing it and not just by reading about it.

Insofar as we can "teach" discernment in a book like this, two questions, I believe, have to be answered: the "what" and the "how." What is discernment? And how does one discern fruitful-ly? In my experience, the crucial question is the "what." In other words, if one has a clear understanding of the *meaning* (and prerequisites) of discernment, then the *mechanics* of discernment will not be too difficult to learn. For this reason, Part I of the present book ("Preparing the Soil") is an attempt to provide a clear understanding of what discernment really is. We find our roots, as in every question of faith, in the scriptures; and so, chapters 1 and 2 explore the place of discernment in the Old and the New Testaments, not with a view to giving a full, technical exegesis (which has already been done by Guillet in the reference cited) but rather in order to provide a feel, a sense for the biblical meaning of discernment.

In early Old Testament times the word never appears, and even the idea of discernment is hardly relevant given the prevalent ideas of God and of human nature. But by the time of John and Paul discernment is a central theme of the apostolic message. Moreover, the whole of the gospels may fruitfully be viewed as a double discernment — by Jesus and about Jesus. If we can grasp the evolution of understanding and experience which made possible this change, we may have a much clearer picture of the place of discernment in the Christian life of today. Chapter 3 seeks to make this picture explicit by exploring the qualities and prerequisites of a truly discerning attitude. What kind of person would one need to be *today* in order to be skilled in discerning the Lord's ongoing revelation of his will for us? What would it mean for us to have the same discerning heart as Jesus himself?

With this background concerning the "what" of discernment, we turn in Part II ("Sowing the Good Seed") to the "how." The classic source is the Rules for the Discernment of Spirits in the *Spiritual Exercises* of St. Ignatius Loyola. Even today these rules, written 450 years ago, are the church's canonical *locus* on discernment. What St. Augustine has done for the problem of evil, or St. Teresa of Avila and St. John of the Cross for the phenomenology of prayer, St. Ignatius, by the grace of the same revealing God, has done for the art of discernment. And so chapters 5 to 7 discuss in detail and apply to our lives his classic rules for beginners in the spiritual life (chapters 5 and 6) and for the mature and committed (chapter 7). But even before we discuss the rules for beginners, who are "sowing the good seed" in Part II, chapter 4 provides the Ignatian foundation for discernment. It is based on a famous section, toward the end of the second week of the *Spiritual Exercises*, wherein Ignatius explains the relationship between discernment and choice, and where he indicates three ways of making a good choice, only one of which is properly discernment.

Part III, which is entitled "A Mixed Harvest," begins (as noted above) with the rules for committed souls. At this time of stability and growth in our relationship with God, the evil spirit has to adopt new, subtler tactics in his effort to subvert the divine will in our lives. Since we have become more sensitive to the sound of his own diabolical voice, he seeks to mimic the voice of the Lord, to confuse us by tempting us under the guise of good. Moreover, as we mature we begin to realize that the "evil spirit" himself has many faces. And so chapter 8, based upon Jesus' parable of the weeds and the wheat growing together until the harvest (Mt 13:24-30), seeks to detect and to explore the various species of weeds (in biblical terms: the world, the flesh and the devil) which grow alongside, and intertwined with, the good wheat in the harvest field of our lives. In terms of Christian discernment and decision making, the weeds and the wheat represent the mix of diverse inspirations and attachments—e.g., the genuine love of God entangled with self-love and self-seeking in even the most generous and zealous of apostles—which complicates the art of discernment even for those who are truly committed and mature.

It is this parable of Jesus which has provided the title for the whole book: *Weeds Among the Wheat.* Ultimately, discernment is crucial in the apostolic life precisely because we live by faith and because there are—and according to Jesus there must be, even until the harvest time—weeds intertwined with the good wheat of our lives. We see here the apostolic dimension of the pray-er's paradox discussed in chapter 2 of *When the Well Runs Dry:* even if the waters of prayer are pure and genuine, some of the flowers in the garden of the good soul do not seem to blossom as they should. And some of the weeds, which the pray-er most regrets and most desires to uproot, seem to be resistant to all his or her efforts and prayers. For the contemplative in action this occasions a double sadness: Not only is she unable to provide for her Lord a weed-free interior garden where he, as Teresa says, can come to take his delight; but the ministry too—the apostolic dimension of our contemplation—is obscured and rendered less fruitful by the weeds that thrive in the harvest field and that entangle the harvester. Chapter 8 seeks to expose these weeds, that we may uproot those which we can uproot, and understand the divine value of those which must be left until the Lord of the harvest sees fit to uproot them.

As chapter 8 implies, there is a close link between the inner maturing of which we spoke in the *Well* and the apostolic maturing of the contemplative in action. Chapter 9 seeks to explore this link: to discover how the "floater" of chapter 6 of the *Well* grows into that habit of discerning love which is the fullness of the apostolic life. Here, I believe, the challenge and the mystery of which I wrote in *Darkness in the Marketplace* finds its resolution. While the present book can be read and understood without a prior knowledge of my earlier books on prayer, in a real sense *Darkness* was itself a book about discernment: It treated of discernment in practice rather than in theory; and it focused on discerning the dark, purifying side of our apostolic life, perhaps because that aspect was uppermost in my own experience at the time. The meaning of the "dark night of the marketplace" seemed in particular need of clarification in my own life, both as a prayer and as a director of others.

Darkness, however, is not the ultimate or the defining reality. The dark night precedes the dawn; and the dry well leads (indeed forces) us to the hidden sources of living water. So too, in our life as apostles, the long and sometimes arduous schooling in the practice of discernment leads to a new sensitivity which we may call "the habit of discerning love." This gift of maturity is the topic of chapter 9. It is, I believe, the real meaning of the beautiful Ignatian phrase "contemplative in action."

Throughout the book we have focused on *personal* discernment. It must be admitted, however, that much current discussion centers on *communal* discernment, on how communities (whether, e.g., religious or parochial or charismatic) can discern God's will for them as a group. And so, in the Epilogue, I explain why I have not treated of communal discernment thus far, and how our treatment of personal discernment can be applied to a community seeking God's will together. It is my belief that a community will not find corporate discernment difficult *if* the individual members are prayerful, discerning persons, and that such communal discernment will be impossible if the members of the community are not persons of prayer and discernment. Our brief treatment of communal discernment, then, concentrates on the specific prerequisites for a community situation, as proposed in a now-classic monograph by Father John Futrell, S.J.

Whether the discernment in question be personal or communal, the real goal is that "habit of discerning love" which leads to true spiritual freedom. And so the Epilogue concludes with a brief discussion of that liberty of spirit which is, perhaps, the Lord's greatest gift to those who have grown into this habit of discerning love. It is a paradox which only lovers can understand: We are most truly free only when we have surrendered our will to the one we love. And this surrender is only possible when we know that we are totally accepted just as we are.

It seems, then, that we have come full circle. We began by stating that it is our call to mature, responsible freedom in our Christian lives which makes discernment so important today. And we conclude with the realization that it is only discerning love which can make us truly free. In our end, it seems, is our beginning. So let us begin!

Part I
Preparing the Soil

Chapter 1
Biblical Beginnings: Good and Evil Prophets

Discernment: The Problem and Its Importance

Not long ago, I gave a seminar on "Prayer and Discernment" to a large group of sisters from England, Ireland and Scotland. The topic was chosen by the sisters themselves, and the response to our days together was uniformly enthusiastic. For me, this was striking confirmation of a belief I had come to, namely, that the art of discernment is both central to the Christian life today and, at the same time, not very well understood even by prayerful and committed Christians.

Growth in prayer and the art of discernment are the two topics about which I am most often asked to speak in the Philippines and on my trips abroad. While the former is widely written about and discussed today, the latter, discernment, remains obscure and mysterious to most pray-ers; and this despite the fact that, as I believe, discernment is the essential link between prayer and the active Christian life, the meeting point of prayer and apostolic action. There are some excellent contemporary articles and books about discernment (to which we shall refer in the course of this book), but they are a mere trickle compared to the flood of good recent literature on prayer. Moreover, some of the best tend to be rather technical and specialized, not easily accessible to the average committed Christian seeking to do God's work in the modern world.

Can the art of discernment be presented in a way that is both accurate and comprehensible to the "lay" reader, to the non-specialist but dedicated priest, sister or layperson? I believe so, although there are formidable obstacles. To begin with, the discerning person must be a praying person — one who takes God seriously and is genuinely concerned with God's involvement in his or her life. Furthermore, one must be able to make certain important distinctions; for example, between working for God and doing God's work, between discerning and deciding, between listening to one's feelings and relying on one's reason — distinctions which, in my experience, are not at all easy to grasp, or accept, experientially.

The *American College Dictionary* (1966) defines the verb "discern" as follows: "1. To perceive by sight or some other sense or by the intellect . . . 2. To distinguish mentally: recognize as distinct or different; discriminate." Thus the ordinary usage of "discern" involves both perceiving and distinguishing or judging. In the case of spiritual discernment also, or "discernment of spirits" as it has been called traditionally, both perception and judgment are important. What is unique to and distinctive of this religious meaning of discernment is the *object* of our perceiving and judging. It is, surprisingly perhaps, our *feelings* that we distinguish and evaluate in spiritual discernment. For this reason it is essential to spiritual discernment that we be in touch with our feelings. How many of us, however, are really so in touch? How many can "name, claim, tame and aim" the feelings within us which are the raw material of discernment? Many people say it is very difficult to know God, since we do not see him, hear him, or touch him as we do another human being. This is true, of course, but I have become convinced that the greatest obstacle to real discernment (and to genuine growth in prayer) is not the intangible nature of God, but, as we shall see in chapter 3, our own lack of self-knowledge — even our *unwillingness* to know ourselves as we truly are. Almost all of us wear masks, not only when facing others but even when looking in the mirror.

These are the factors which make discernment a fairly rare art, and the idea of discernment difficult to grasp. At the same time, however, it is the key to a genuinely Christian life and the difficulties are not insuperable for those who sincerely desire to grow. In essence discernment is an art, not a science; it is learned by doing, by trial and error. And it is a gift, not primarily the fruit of personal effort, but God's gift to those who love and are loved by him.

As art and gift, discernment cannot be taught; but we can explain the dimensions of the gift. We can indicate, as we hope to do in this chapter and the second, the meaning and central place of discernment in the scriptural revelation. Moreover, we are fortunate in that the principal charism of St. Ignatius Loyola, and of the Society of Jesus which he founded, is the "discernment of spirits." In the two brief sets of rules for discernment which are at the heart of his *Spiritual Exercises,* Ignatius (or rather, the Lord through Ignatius) has given to the church the fundamental guidelines of authentic discernment. These rules are eminently practical and down-to-earth, as we shall see in chapters 4 and following. Their very brevity can pose a problem, and we shall try to put some flesh on their bones by way of explanation and example. But we shall do so, I hope, without losing any of the concreteness of St. Ignatius himself. Whatever we say of discernment, we should never lose our solid grounding in the marketplace of Christian life and action.

The God of Early Israel

We begin, then, where all good Christian teaching begins: in the scripture. The Old Testament rarely, if ever, uses the word "discernment." More surprising still is the fact that the idea of discernment is not found until a fairly late point in the history of Israel. To understand why this is so, it might be good to start by indicating a basic problem: who God is for man. There are, as I see it, three distinct possible views of God, views which we might label "the watchmaker," "the puppeteer," and "the father of adult children." Let me explain.

If God is seen as the watchmaker, then no true discernment is possible. He made the world, as the watchmaker produces the watch, but his involvement with his creation ends when he has finished making it. I have a watch which was given to me at ordination in 1963. It is beautiful in its simplicity and has kept almost perfect time for 20 years now. In all that time, I have had it in for repairs or cleaning only two or three times. If you asked me about the watchmaker, I would say he must have been a very skillful artisan. I am sure he existed, and I know he was good at his craft. But I have no idea who he was, nor do I even know whether he is still living. He put something of himself into my watch, but once he had finished his work, and the watch left his shop, he no longer had any direct involvement with it. So it is with the "watchmaker" idea of God: He created the world and left the stamp of his skill and being on it, but he no longer has any direct connection with his creation. From that creation, we could learn something about him (as I could about the maker of my watch by considering the artistry and accuracy of his handiwork), but we could not know him personally or enter into a direct personal relationship with him.

Such is the God of modern deists: a real but unknowable cause of creation. To ask what such a God desires of us — to try to *discern* his will in our lives today — would be as useless as asking what the watchmaker would like me to do with my watch today. I might assume that he would want me to care for it, and to keep it properly cleaned; but I could never be sure. It is possible that he detested his work, and would be happy to see all his creations destroyed. This may be unlikely, but one thing is certain: I can never ask him! Nor would it make much sense to spend time worrying about what the absent, and perhaps dead, watchmaker would like me to do with my watch. For better or worse, it is my responsibility now.

As we said, with a watchmaker-God discernment would be neither meaningful nor possible. If, on the other hand, God is seen as a puppeteer, then discernment is unnecessary. If God is directly and totally involved in his creation in such a way that he holds all the strings and manipulates persons and events the way a puppet master controls his puppets, then we are not free. We don't need to discover his will, since he is going to bring it about whether we like it or not. To vary the metaphor, we would be pawns on the chessboard of life moved about by the divine chess master. Pawns and puppets have no need to seek to discover what is expected of them.

The watchmaker-God of deism is, as we noted, a modern phenomenon, the fruit of the rationalism of recent centuries when technology began to believe it could manage, and understand, everything by itself. As far as I know, there were no deist writers propounding a "watchmaker" view of God in primitive societies.

Certainly God was no watchmaker for the Old Testament patriarchs and prophets. He was involved with the ongoing development and destiny of his creation from the very beginning in the Garden of Eden (Gn 3). But the puppeteer-God is a very ancient conception — probably, in fact, the most ancient idea of God. Carried to the extreme, this view would completely negate human freedom and responsibility. Such an extreme, however, would require a fairly sophisticated level of theological reflection. More often, for ordinary people and for primitive societies, man's responsibility and God's absolute dominion would coexist in an uneasy tension. This, it seems, was the case for the early Israelites. King Saul, for example, is described as moved — possessed — by good and evil spirits at crucial moments in his reign; yet he was praised and blamed for his actions. Inconsistent as this may seem, it is a very common attitude even today. How often I hear people say: "I sinned and God is angry with me; and yet how could I help it? I begged him not to let me meet my married lover again." Or: "Why did God allow my son to go astray? How have I offended him, that he did not answer my prayer?" Although it may not be realized, the God who makes sons good (or bad) and manipulates meetings with illicit lovers is really a puppeteer, a chess master.

For our purposes, the important point is that discernment does not make sense in such a world-view, with its contradictory blend of freedom and fatalism. This is true especially when the dominant mood is fatalistic, as seems to have been true in ancient Israel. In the classic work on the history of discernment, Jacques Guillet, S.J., writes:

> . . . in the most ancient texts we may not yet speak of discernment of spirits for two reasons. First of all, the action of these spirits (good and evil) is so overwhelming and powerful that it seems impossible for the one experiencing the action to resist it. Doubtless, he does not lose his personality. It is the same Saul whom the good spirit makes a marvelous chief (1 Sm 11:6), while the evil spirit turns him into a cruel and suspicious tyrant (16:14-23); all the while Saul remains the man who merits praise for his bravery and condemnation for his unjustifiable jealousy. Nevertheless, in both situations he

is given over to one stronger than himself.[1]

The second reason given by Guillet for the absence of any idea of discernment in the ancient Old Testament texts is that, for the Israelites, "both good and evil spirits have the same origin. They come from the Lord God, although the former show forth his plan of salvation and the latter will lead his adversaries to ruin (Jgs 9:23; 1 Sm 16:14-23; 18:10; 19:9; 2 Kgs 19:7; Is 19:14; 29:10)." We shall have to discuss later the meaning of "spirits" in this context, and the distinction between good and evil spirits. For the moment, though, the important point is that every impulse, whether good or evil, was seen as coming from God and as overpowering man. In such a world-view, God is virtually the puppeteer and the human being's discerning response to him has little meaning.

The God of the Prophets

As time passed, however, the great religious figures of Israel began to see their relationships to Yahweh in a new light. Fatalism gave way to a sense of personal responsibility and God came to be seen as a friend and a father — a father of adult children, we might say. What I mean by this is that the father imagery is open to different interpretations depending on whether the children are young or adult. Young children are more than puppets, since they relate to their parents in love and they do have minds of their own. But they do not have the experience or the maturity to share in making the important decisions touching the family or even touching their own lives. Gradually, and usually awkwardly and painfully, they begin to assert their right to do so.

In most families the transition from small child to adult daughter or son is a difficult one. Sometimes it is never accomplished and the children, tied forever by mama's apron strings, never become mature adults. Sometimes it is accomplished only at the cost of alienation and bitterness that can last a

---

1 *Discernment of Spirits* (Collegeville, Minnesota: The Liturgical Press, 1970) p. 19. This is the English translation by Sr. Innocentia Richards of the classic article from the *Dictionnaire de Spiritualite Ascetique et Mystique:* "Discernement des Esprits," by Jacques Guillet *et al.*

lifetime. Ideally, however, the transition does take place, successfully if not gracefully, and the relationship between parent and son or daughter is transformed. They now meet as adults, as friends, in some sense as equals. Since friendship demands equality, it is perhaps only now that parent and child can meet as real friends. The daughter or son is grateful for the gifts of nature and nurture and reverences the wisdom of age and experience, but is also autonomous, capable of mature reflection and action, and responsible for the direction of his or her own life. The mature parent finds fulfillment and success precisely in the responsible independence of the child come of age.

The process we have been describing is both the most challenging and the most rewarding aspect of being a parent. But can we apply it analogously to our relationship with God? It might seem strange to say that we can; after all, God is the supreme Lord of our lives. Would it make sense to speak of our becoming autonomous before *him,* of our meeting him adult to adult? It seems strange to think of our relationship to God himself in those terms.[2] It is true, I think, that there is a vast difference between our mature relationship to God and our adult relationship to our parents. But Jesus did teach us to call God "Father"! And he clearly implied (and St. Paul expressly stated in 1 Corinthians 3:1-3[3]) that this relationship to God as our Father is an evolving, maturing one.

Jesus uses human fatherhood as an analogy for our mature relationship to God, and like every analogy it implies both difference and similarity. The fact that the differences are great should not blind us to the real similarity. For our purposes, this similarity in the analogy of maturing children involves discernment. St. Paul, in the letter just cited (1 Cor 2:15), defines the "spiritual" (mature) man as one who "is able to judge the value of

---

2 Those who are familiar with *When the Well Runs Dry* and *Darkness in the Marketplace* could readily object that such a conception seems to conflict with the very purpose of the dry well or the dark night: to let go of our own attachments and controls, to allow God to be truly Lord of our lives.

3 "Brothers, I myself was unable to speak to you as people of the Spirit: I treated you as sensual men, still infants in Christ. What I fed you with was milk, not solid food, for you were not ready for it; and indeed, you are still not ready for it since you are still unspiritual" (Cf. 1 Thes 2:7 and 1 Pt 2:2).

everything, and (whose) own value is not to be judged by other men." In a beautiful passage the author of the letter to the Hebrews says,

> On this subject (the priesthood of Jesus) we have many things to say, and they are difficult to explain because you have grown so slow at understanding. Really, when you should by this time have become masters, you need someone to teach you all over again the elementary principles of interpreting God's oracles; you have gone back to needing milk, and not solid food. Truly, anyone who is still living on milk cannot digest the doctrine of righteousness because he is still a baby. Solid food is for mature men with minds trained by practice to discern between good and bad (Heb 5:11-14).

The mature Christian, then, is one who can discern, one who does not have to be spoon-fed with explicit instructions for every situation, with detailed guidelines from "Papa." There is thus a valid point to our analogy of the father of adult children! In the Old Testament, as we noted above, this call to maturity before God only gradually dawns on the consciousness of Israel. When it does so — when personal responsibility before Yahweh begins to be important — the idea of discernment (although not the word itself) becomes prominent in the prophetic writings. As Guillet notes, this is because the voice, the will of God, is recognized as obscure and mysterious. Not every "spirit" is God's spirit. There are other voices competing with his:

> Along with the divine voice there is another voice, the voice of sin (Gn 4:7), the voice of Satan, God's opponent. This voice, likewise, is somewhat mysterious. Now it seems to arise from the heart of man, to express his own desire (Gn 6:5; 11:4; Ex 32:9; Dt 32:5, 20; Ps 95:10), again it is clear that the voice does not come from the man himself, but from a source that is disquieting — more rational and stronger than he, more tenacious, more aware of his plans, better informed than he regarding the tendencies of his own heart, and, apparently, capable of understanding divine purposes (Gn 3).[4]

Life becomes more complex as we mature. A simple, blind, childlike following of clear commands is no longer possible. God's

---

4 Guillet, *op. cit.*, pp. 17-18.

being and revelation are much more mysterious than when our faith was that of a child; the well of simple verities runs dry, or at least the water becomes much more cloudy. As we move out of our sheltered home into the darkness of the marketplace, there are many more voices competing for our attention with the Lord's (and often mimicking his). Guillet describes the situation thus (p. 18):

> Man is plunged into a threefold darkness. God commands without being seen; Satan conceals himself, suggests more than he affirms, proposes more than he demands. . . . Finally, there is the darkness in man himself who is incapable of seeing his own heart clearly, incapable of grasping completely the seriousness of his actions and the results deriving from them (Ex 32:21; 2 Sm 12:7).

In this "threefold darkness" man is challenged to choose and to act:

> Choice for this man is not only the selection of this or that mode of acting; it requires, also, the identification of the voices he hears. Therefore, he must make a discriminating judgment — and that is "discernment."

Discerning Authentic Prophecy

In the Old Testament, perhaps the most important application of discernment concerns the recognition of true and false prophets. Many prophets appeared in Israel during the centuries when the monarchy was strong. Frequently they were in opposition to one another, making conflicting prophecies and urging contrary courses of action. How, then, were the Jewish people and their leaders to determine which prophets were truly speaking God's word to them? Over the centuries certain criteria emerged. Guillet cites six such norms for authentic prophecy — in effect six criteria for discerning who is truly speaking the word of God.[5] We may summarize these as follows:

1. Prophecies of misfortune are more likely to be authentic than prophecies of good fortune. The principle here seems to be that favorable prophecies could easily be a way of courting

---

5 *Ibid.*, pp. 21-23. Guillet gives numerous scriptural citations illustrating the application of each of the criteria.

popularity and pandering to the desires of the hearers. On the other hand, there is little natural reason to prophesy bad luck. Even today a political leader who tells us we must trim our sails or tighten our belts is much less likely to win elections or popularity. Thus one speaking in this way is more likely to be speaking from sincere conviction.

2. Authentic prophecy is confirmed from the prediction of "signs" which actually do come to pass. It is good to note here that to prophesy does not mean, in the first instance, "to predict" but rather to speak on behalf of another. The prophet was one who spoke in the name of Yahweh. When we take prophecy today to connote prediction, we are focusing on an accidental feature of the prophetic vocation. But we are not entirely mistaken: The prophet did make predictions, though merely as a means of confirming the authenticity of his divine call. When Jesus says "even if you refuse to believe in me, at least believe in the work I do" (Jn 10:38), he is using his "signs" as a validation of his doctrine and mission. Similarly, when John the Baptist doubts Jesus' messiahship, the Lord appeals to his works, confident that John will be reassured by them even though he is troubled by Jesus' mode of preaching and acting:

> Jesus answered, "Go back and tell John what you hear and see; the blind see again and the lame walk, lepers are cleansed and the deaf hear, the dead are raised to life and the Good News is proclaimed to the poor; and happy is the man who does not lose faith in me" (Mt 11:4-6).

3. Even more important than the above criteria is the test of fidelity to the fundamental faith of Israel. In fact, even signs and wonders successfully performed are no sure guarantee of the prophet's authenticity; the devil, too, can perform miracles. As we shall see in part III of this book, consoling events and experiences are, unfortunately, not a certain sign of God's presence and influence. That is why Jesus also took pains to show that he had not come to destroy the Mosaic law (revelation) but to fulfill it (Mt 5:17). And even the Israelites, at an early stage in the development of the doctrine of discernment, realized this:

If some prophet arises among you or a dreamer of dreams

gives you a sign or a wonder and the sign or wonder comes to pass, and if he says, "Let us go after other gods which you have not known, and let us serve them," you shall not listen to the words of that prophet, to the dreamer of dreams.[6]

God is faithful and cannot contradict himself. The doctrine of revelation — our grasp of it — can and does evolve; but evolution can never mean contradiction. If the prophet does contradict the basic faith of Israel or the church, he cannot be moved by the Spirit of God. It is worth acknowledging, though, that it is not easy to determine whether creative religious thinkers (like Isaiah, the author of Job, or Jesus himself) are really contradicting the revelation, or merely challenging the accepted and distorted understanding of that revelation. Teilhard de Chardin and Martin Luther King are contemporary witnesses to this difficulty!

4. For this reason, the life witness of the prophet will be as important as his soundness of doctrine. Guillet makes the interesting observation that this behavioral criterion is valid at least negatively: "It may not be absolutely certain that an irreproachable prophet is speaking in the name of God, but the false prophet is always betrayed by a sinful life."[7] I suspect the Pharisees may be a case in point here. That is, while we sometimes tend to see them as villains, to their contemporaries their moral and religious lives probably appeared irreproachable. They exemplify a piety, an "outstanding" religious zeal which is misleading, and which we have come to call "pharisaical." By contrast, a sinful life can never be a mark of a genuine prophet: a diabolical Adolf Hitler or a fanatical Jim Jones, whatever his power over people and events in Guyana, could not possibly be an authentic prophet.

5. All the above criteria — misfortune, signs, doctrine, behavior — are visible and external. The fifth criterion, though, is the intention of the prophet. Does he or she act in order to curry favor and win power, or to convert people to the living God? Guillet calls this criterion "more delicate," precisely because, I

---

6 Dt 13:23. Quoted by Guillet, p. 21.

7 Guillet, p. 22.

think, it is interior and can be gauged only by the visible phenomena described above.

6. Similarly interior is the sixth and final criterion enumerated by Guillet: the prophet's own experience of his or her prophetic call. For the prophet himself this is "definitive" and decisive. And for this reason we find an inaugural vision described by virtually all of the prophets (e.g., Is 6; Jer 1:4-10; Ex 3 for Moses; Hos 1-3). It is the experience which set them apart, cleansed their lips, made them God's spokesmen. While it cannot be directly perceived or verified by their hearers, this experience is crucial for the prophets themselves. It is the moment when they were captured by the living God; whatever good may have followed in their lives derives from this initial transforming experience. The concrete results are the fruit and confirmation of their initial encounter with the living God of Israel.

Conclusion

These, then, are the six Old Testament norms for discerning the authenticity or genuineness of a prophet's vocation. They helped the Jewish people to test the prophetic claims of those men who professed to be instructing them and commanding them in Yahweh's name. Although the term "discernment" is not yet found, and the scope of discernment is rather narrow (compared to the New Testament idea, which we shall consider shortly), our brief review of the practice of discernment in Israel has yielded some important insights.

We have seen, first, that God is involved with his creation. He is not a watchmaker who sets the world in motion and then abandons it to its own inner dynamic. Nor does he wish to be a puppet master, manipulating creation to his own ends in a deterministic way. He *is* the Father of small children, but it is not his desire that his children remain forever immature and dependent in a childish or servile way. His goal, for Israel and for us, is maturity, a mature and responsible relationship with him — the relationship of adult children with their Father and friend. We are to be "no longer servants but friends," to paraphrase John 15:15.

Secondly, God's involvement in our history is often obscure and tricky to interpret. This is especially true as we move from childhood to maturity. In the Garden of Eden God's will for Adam and Eve was simple and clear-cut, even though the reasons for his will were not clear. As time passed, however, Yahweh chose to speak to his people through human beings rather than directly as in the garden. In doing so he chose to risk distortion of his word and infidelity on the part of his all-too-human spokesmen — a risk which God took, I believe, precisely because of his desire that men and women be mature partners in the work of salvation and redemption. The Lord could have managed history much more effectively if he regularly intervened directly and "miraculously." Even today many good people would prefer this arrangement. It would require less faith and less struggle on our part. But it would not be the way for the Father to bring his beloved children to maturity.

Finally, and as a consequence of what we have just said, the mature man or woman has a responsibility to judge, to discriminate between authentic and inauthentic "voices" or spokesmen of Yahweh. The Lord does care about our lives. He is involved in our history. But he does not force his will upon us. And he chooses to work through human agents who can distort or misinterpret his guiding word.

For the Israelites, discernment was focused upon the problem of authentic prophecy. At Jesus' coming, as we shall see in the next chapter, the prophetic vocation will be fulfilled and transformed. As a result, each of the above three points — that God is involved in human history, that his involvement is often mysterious and obscure, and that consequently we have a responsibility to discern his word — will be developed and clarified. But it is clear already that the God of the Judaeo-Christian tradition is, and wishes to be, neither a watchmaker nor a puppeteer but a father of adult children. His choice to relate to us in this way is the foundation of all Christian discernment.

Practicum Question

(Note: Since discernment is an art and thus learned by doing, I have found it helpful in my course on discernment to conclude each presentation with a concrete question applying what has been discussed to our own lives. You might find it profitable to do the same as you read this book. My own comments on the questions will be found in the appendix.)

For chapter one, consider the following: Today as much as ever, the mature Christian is called upon to "discern" the prophets of our times, and to judge which of them should be accepted as authentic spokesmen of God. Which of the six Old Testament criteria for authentic prophecy would you consider most helpful in discerning a genuine prophet today? (You could answer the question in a general way, or you could consider some specific prophetic figure like Gandhi or Martin Luther King or Pope John XXIII.)

Chapter 2
Jesus Discerning and Discerned

We have discovered that the Old Testament writers were moving toward an understanding of God and man which would entail discernment. The God of Israel was involved in the history of his creation. He was not a watchmaker-God who fashioned things and people and then left them to their own devices and to the natural laws of their being. Moreover, his personal involvement was mysterious and obscure; it left room for human freedom and it was manifested through human agents who could distort and confuse his message in the transmission. In addition, there seemed to be other "spirit" voices at work, competing with Yahweh and trying to mislead his people by mimicking his voice. Because of this obscurity, men and women were called to live by faith and not by clear vision: They had to make judgments about Yahweh's will for them, discriminating among the various inspirations and prophetic voices which all purported to be from the Lord. In short (although the word was not yet used), they had to *discern*.

Father of Adult Children

This call to discernment was real, and yet the common Israelite understanding of God was not yet sufficiently mature (from the New Testament point of view) to allow for a fully developed doctrine of discernment. There was still something mechanical about the way Old Testament people read the mind of God. That is, external signs and authority were much more important than the inner inspirations of their own hearts. The Book of Job is perhaps the most beautiful testimony to the problem which Israel thus faced: Job suffered and so Job must have sinned and must repent. According to his friends, who represent orthodox Jewish theology at the time, Job's external misery is a clear indication that Yahweh is displeased with him. When he protests that his own conscience does not rebuke him — that he cannot repent what he is unaware of — his friends take this for a sign of stubbornness and pride. If he suffers, he must have sinned; and the only solution is to repent and do penance for *whatever* it is that has provoked Yahweh. That Job's conscience does not reproach him proves nothing, except that man's mind cannot comprehend the judgments of God.

The author of the Book of Job uses this debate to register his protest against the prevailing understanding of God's ways with human beings. Through the *persona* of Job he insists that he cannot accept such an arbitrary and capricious God. The God of the friends of Job is perhaps not a puppeteer, since Job is free to surrender or to remain obstinate. But the picture presented is of an absolute monarch or a father of small children: God's ways with men are not to be questioned since he is so far beyond us in intelligence and power. Ours is not to understand but simply to accept and submit.

It may have struck the reader that this picture of God, rejected by Job and his creator, is not far from the idea which many Christians still have. It has, in fact, been canonized in predestinarian traditions such as those of Calvin and John Knox, for whom God works his will with men and women inexorably and inevitably. And it has led, in one development of the Lutheran tradition, to the idea that what is most unreasonable to human beings is more likely to be God's will, since "God's foolishness is wiser than human wisdom, and God's weakness is stronger than human strength" (1 Cor 1:25).

But the God-image of Job's friends is often found implicitly even in Christian traditions that stress human freedom and personal responsibility. After all, the above quotation is from St. Paul and is part of the biblical revelation; and it is followed by 22 verses in which Paul draws a sharp contrast between human philosophy and the wisdom of the cross. Thus every follower of the Crucified must acknowledge that God's ways are not our natural ways. The problem, of course, is whether we take this to mean that God's ways contradict our human understanding or rather transcend it.

Can God make a square circle? For St. Thomas Aquinas, and for all who, like him, see human intelligence as a created participation in the divine, the answer has to be "no." What is contradictory for our created minds cannot be made truth by the Mind in whose wisdom we participate. We may be mistaken, of course. We may use our reason incorrectly and draw erroneous conclusions. But insofar as we do use our intelligence correctly, we can never come to conclusions which God's understanding contradicts. On the other hand, our "philosophy" may, indeed surely will, fall far short of the whole truth. God's wisdom will inevitably transcend — go far beyond — what we have been able to grasp humanly. A person steeped in the wisdom of the cross can ultimately realize that Calvary was the only way. Naturally speaking, he or she could never have discovered the way of the cross; but once it has been revealed, and the revelation has become part of our very person, we see that it does not contradict our philosophy even though it expands our horizons immeasurably, transcends all that our philosophy could ever have imagined.

The point we are making here is a bit "heavy," but I hope the reader will have the patience to reread and digest it. For there is another view with fateful implications: the view that God *can* make a square circle, that everything, even what is contradictory for us, is possible to him, and we can set no rational limits to what he might do. If this were true, I fear we could never escape the picture of the absolute monarch or the father of small children. That, in effect, would make genuine discernment impossible. Many people who have never reflected on their basic assumptions do operate from such a world view. Many of them feel they can be truly free, truly human only by eliminating God from their lives — a God who, as Sartre felt, is a threat to their full humanity. Many others, who do desire to be truly religious and God-centered, feel they can do so only by losing their own personhood.

These two responses — rejection and slavish submission — both spring from a view of God as very demanding and, as it were, antihuman. Sartrean existentialism has popularized the notion that "God" must die in history if man is to be fully human — that man can be truly free and responsible only if he rejects a God who suffocates him and reduces him to a helpless child. But such a reaction could gain wide acceptance, I believe, only if the God of religious people actually seemed to make such demands on his devotees. This has been the case all too often; for example, religious congregations' ideas of common life and obedience have often been distorted in such a way as to canonize the annihilation of personality.

St. Benedict introduced common life as a corrective for the eccentric individualism of some desert spirituality. He felt, after many years of life as a hermit, that holiness was not to be achieved by extreme solitary practices of prayer and penance but by living with great love an ordinary life in community. This was common life: the sanctification of the ordinary.[1] But over the centuries, and down to our own time, the ideal of common life was distorted; it came to mean a sort of faceless "long black line" where every sister was ideally indistinguishable from every other, and where the norm for a good priest celebrating Mass was (as I myself was taught only 20 years ago) that when he left the altar the congregation would not have noticed who the celebrant was. These examples may seem bizarre and exaggerated today, with our stress on the unique personality and the psycho-emotional needs of every person and the need to make every liturgical celebration a truly human and communal experience. Bizarre they may be, but they are not exaggerated, and their effects still linger on in many of us who were formed, or deformed, in a depersonalizing, mechanical tradition of common life.

Similarly, obedience, which in Jesus' own life was a consuming passion for his father and his father's will, became institutionalized as a blind, unthinking, even robotized following of whatever authority decided in the name of God. St. Ignatius Loyola, in his famous letter on obedience, canonized "blind obedience," but only as the term of a long process of dialogue and discerning by superior and subject. Teresa of Avila, in *The Interior Castle* (Fifth Mansions, ch. 3), says that "union of wills" is

---

1 George Lane, S.J.'s *Christian Spirituality* (reissue, Loyola University Press, 1984) gives a very good summary of the stages of development of Christian spirituality. Also excellent is the fuller treatment in Jordan Aumann, O.P., *History of Spirituality* (Manila: St. Paul Publications, 1979).

the only type of union essential to holiness. But Teresa was the most forceful and sensible of women; the union of wills which she places at the heart of holiness is a union of the will of God with a dynamic, passionate, fully alive human will. It is the "passionate inwardness" of which Kierkegaard speaks. For them—Ignatius, Teresa and Kierkegaard—one does not become a saint by becoming a robot but by harnessing the full potential of one's personality and, to mix our metaphors, channeling it to the all-consuming goal of the love and service of God.

Unfortunately, though perhaps inevitably, the ideal of obedience, no less than that of common life, became seriously distorted over the centuries. Blind obedience often was used, and understood, as an abortive device—a means for terminating any questioning or personal initiative. To ask questions and make suggestions, which St. Ignatius saw as an integral part of the discerning process of obedience, was seen instead as a failure in religious virtue. The "blindness" which he recommended as the term of a process—as the ideal when it seems clear that God's will is contrary to my understanding—became instead the starting point of the process of obedience. When Jesus, in the Garden of Gethsemane, said "Father, not my will but yours be done," he had already dialogued with the Father and expressed freely his own human understanding of what was best. Only when he had begged the Father in prayer three times to find a "better" way, and when it seemed inexplicably clear that Calvary was the Father's way, only then did Jesus "blindly" surrender to what the Father willed.

As this reference to Gethsemane indicates, I believe that the robotized ideals of common life and obedience are far from the New Testament vision of God and man. The Sartrean "death of God" reaction to religion may have a valid point regarding institutionalized religion. But Jesus, in his confrontations with the Pharisees (e.g., Jn 5,7 and 8), proclaimed that such is far removed from the reality which he knew and came to reveal. In his eyes, the institutionalization of obedience and the automaton concept of discipline in pharisaism was a distortion of the Old Testament revelation (Mt 15:1-20). For him, religion is interior (Mt 6:1-18) and God is "Father" (Mt 6:2, 9, 14, 15, etc.), a Father to whom he relates, and teaches us to relate, as an adult son or daughter (cf., Jesus' priestly prayer in Jn:17, and his praise of John the Baptist in Mt 11:2-19).

Discernment Lived and Evaluated

Hence the three points which we noted as emerging in the Old Testament revelation — God involved in our history, man as responsible and mature, and the consequent importance of discernment in living authentically before God — are realized in a deeper and fuller sense in the life and teaching of Jesus. This is beautifully revealed in both the gospels and the epistles: in the latter explicitly, since a theory of discernment is elaborated in the epistles of John and of Paul; and in the gospels not in theory but in practice, without the word "discernment" being used. Guillet expresses the contrast in this way:

> The expression "discernment of spirits" appears in the epistles (1 Cor 12:10; 1 Jn 4:1), but not in the gospels, although the evangelists are aware of it. Occupied in recounting the words and actions of Jesus, they care little about elaborating a doctrine. On the other hand, the epistles, faced with the problems raised in the Christian communities, give more place to both the principles and the theory of discernment of spirits. Speaking broadly, we may say the discernment of spirits is *lived* in the gospels and *evaluated* in the epistles.[2]

The lived experience of discernment in the gospels is all the more striking because they reveal to us a *double* discernment taking place: Jesus' own discernment of his identity and mission, and the disciples' discernment of Jesus' call to them, of his identity and mission as it touches their lives. Guillet calls the former "infallible" and the latter "groping":

> When Jesus appears, immediately he obliges all those he meets to question themselves on the subject of whence he comes, on the spirit that moves him, and the power he has at his disposal. The synoptics (Matthew, Mark and Luke) present his appearance as the juncture of two ways, and might we not say, of two discernments. On the one hand, Jesus' infallible discernment of what he is and

---

2 Guillet, *op. cit.*, p. 30. Emphasis added.

what he has come to do; on the other hand, a groping discernment on the part of those he came to activate, to clarify and to sustain . . . to awaken (to) that perception which, through faith, finally detects the mystery of his person and his mission.[3]

Jesus Discerning

Each of these discernments — that of Jesus and that of the first disciples — is important to our own understanding of the meaning and place of discernment in our lives. First, Jesus himself discerns "infallibly." Guillet's conjunction of "infallible" and "discernment" with reference to Jesus himself is quite mysterious. Recall that we have said that discernment presupposes obscurity and unclarity about what God is really saying to us. Father Edward Malatesta, S.J., defines discernment as follows:

> By the discernment of *spirits* is meant the process by which we examine, in the light of faith and in the connaturality of love, the nature of the spiritual states we experience in ourselves and in others. The purpose of such examination is to decide, as far as possible, which of the movements we experience lead to the Lord and to a more perfect service of him and our brothers, and which deflect us from this goal.[4]

We shall have to explain more fully the meaning of "spirits" in part II; but note for now that there are *diverse* spirits at work, conflicting inspirations which seem to come from God. This is why discernment presupposes obscurity or ambiguity. If God's voice and God's will is transparently clear, then there is nothing to discern.

To return, then, to Jesus, it is quite puzzling to affirm that he discerned infallibly. If this means that everything was perfectly clear to him from the beginning, as we usually assume — that from Mary's womb he knew clearly and fully in his human con-

---

3 *Ibid*, p. 32.

4 From the Introduction, p. 9, to *Discernment of Spirits* by Guillet *et al*. The phrase, "connaturality of love," is a beautiful inheritance of the scholastic tradition in theology. It refers to that knowledge which comes not from reasoning and analysis but from long-lived experience of one we love. It is the knowledge a wife appeals to when she says, "I *know* my husband. He would never cheat."

sciousness who he was and what he was to do and suffer—then it is difficult to see how we could speak of discernment at all in Jesus' case. Wht would there be for him to discern if God's will were clear at all times? What obscurity or ambiguity would there be?

We could, of course, simply deny that Jesus discerned. Perhaps Guillet uses the word "discernment" loosely and incorrectly with reference to Jesus? While this is the usual and "traditional" picture most of us have—that Jesus, in his humanity, knew everything and never had the doubts or endured the struggles which we have and endure—I believe it is incorrect and incompatible with what scripture tells us of his human experience.

Matthew (4:1-11) and Luke (4:1-13) both describe Jesus' three temptations in the desert at the beginning of his public ministry. The passages are striking since they reveal him as the new Moses or the new Israel. Each time he is tempted by Satan, Jesus quotes from passages in Deuteronomy where Moses is reminding the Israelites of their great failures during the desert years, and warning them to be wary of the devil's temptations in the future. Jesus is the new Israel: Where she failed Yahweh, he has triumphed over Satan. And in his victory she is redeemed. The passage is thus highly symbolic, and for this reason we might be inclined to say that "temptation" should not be applied too literally to Jesus' experience. The author of the Epistle to the Hebrews, however, is quite explicit when he says:

> Since in Jesus, the Son of God, we have the supreme high priest who has gone through to the highest heaven, we must never let go of the faith that we have professed. For it is not as if we have a high priest who was incapable of feeling our weaknesses with us; but we have one *who has been tempted in every way that we are, though he is without sin.* Let us be confident, then, in approaching the throne of grace, that we shall have mercy from him and find grace when we are in need of help" (Heb 4:14-16. Emphasis added).

For the author of Hebrews, the basis of our confidence and hope is precisely that Jesus, our high priest, has been tempted in every way that we are. He goes on to describe Jesus as compassionate because, like every high priest, "He can sympathize with those who are ignorant or uncertain because he too lives in the limitations of weakness" (5:2). While it is difficult to say precisely how the author would apply this to the sinless Jesus, he does tell us shortly thereafter: "Although he was Son, he learnt to obey through suffering; but having been made perfect, he became for all who obey him the source of eternal salvation" (5:8-9). These latter quotations bring out my reason for discussing above the fact that Jesus was tempted. For *could* we be tempted if everything was clear to us? It seems not. There will be no temptations in heaven, since it would not make any sense for the devil to tempt those who see God face to face. What could he possibly entice them with? Or how could he possibly confuse those who see everything with the vision of God? That ignorance and uncertainty to which Hebrews 5:2 refers, would seem to be necessary if one is to be tempted or even be capable of being tempted.

It may seem surprising to apply this to Jesus, even given the passages we have cited from the gospels and from Hebrews. But many passages from scripture seem to portray such a "human" Jesus. Luke tells us, in 2:52, that Jesus returned to Nazareth with his parents after the finding in the Temple and "increased in wisdom, in stature and in favor with God and men." It is difficult to comprehend how one who knew everything from the beginning could grow in wisdom. Similarly, to cite just one or two striking passages, Matthew 26 (v. 36-46) describes Jesus' Gethsemane experience as a real agony of uncertainty and doubt. Three times Jesus prays: "Father . . . if it is possible let this cup pass me by. Nevertheless, let it be as you, not I, would have it." And in John 12:27 (which seems to be John's transposition of the agony event) Jesus says:

"Now my soul is troubled.
What shall I say:
Father, save me from this hour?
But it was for this very reason
    that I have come to this hour.
Father, glorify your name!"

Although the Jesus of St. John's gospel might be said to be the most "divine" of all the gospels, nonetheless even in John we find indications that he was growing in his realization of his identity and mission.

To young people today, this picture of a Jesus who is close to our human experience seems quite normal. But to those of us raised in an earlier age, it can be rather shocking. Although the church documents have surprisingly little to say on the question of Jesus' human consciousness, most of us have been accustomed to think of him and believe in him as very different from, and far beyond, us. To say that he learned as we do, was tempted as we are, lived somehow in the same obscurity of faith as ourselves — all this seems incompatible with our faith in his divinity. If we take Hebrews 4 quite literally, would we not be saying that Jesus became divine only at the end of his human life? Or, worse still, that he was not divine at all but simply a very great man?

Both of these views clearly contradict the church's faith. We cannot say that Jesus was *merely* human, nor that he only gradually became divine. How then can we understand the affirmation that he lived in the obscurity of faith and was subject to temptation just as we are, and still not compromise his divinity? I have found the following analogy helpful. When Prince Charles and Princess Diana of England had a son, the infant prince became second in the line of succession to the British throne, after his father. In fact, if Queen Elizabeth and Prince Charles were to die tomorrow, young William would be king. He may not be totally aware of his royal identity today, and yet he is the heir to the throne. As he grows and matures he will gradually come to realize his identity. Soon, he will sense that he is different from his playmates; later, that he is the "heir apparent," of royal blood. By the time he is 20 he will have a much clearer understanding of what this means; by 30 it will be clearer still. It is not his identity that changes, but his understanding, his conscious grasp of who he is. From the day of his birth he is of royal blood, the heir apparent. But only as the years pass will he come to a fully conscious awareness of this unique identity.

I believe that Jesus' situation was similar to that of Prince William. From the moment of the incarnation he was, as our faith clearly affirms, truly the Son of God as well as the son of Mary. But still, scripture tells us, he was tempted as we are, grew in wisdom and grace, learned obedience through suffering.

Unlike William, Jesus had both a divine and a human consciousness, and in his divine consciousness all truth was grasped fully from eternity. In his human consciousness, however, there must have been need to grow and discover as we do, and as Prince William must. It is, of course, profoundly mysterious that Jesus had both a divine and a complete human nature. We can never comprehend by reason how such a conjunction is possible. But we cannot resolve the mystery by denying one of the truths revealed. Jesus is truly divine and truly human, and his divinity does not, cannot swallow up his humanity. In this humanity, he grew and learned and was tempted. If our analogy to Prince William is valid, it was by this very human process that he gradually came to a full, conscious possession of his divinity, to a full awareness of who he was and had always been.

In this way we can see how Guillet could say that Jesus truly discerned. Yet, equally clearly, there is something different about the gospel Jesus: He is shown to have a unique, unerring sense of his identity and mission, especially in passages like his confrontation with the Pharisees (Jn 5, 7 and 8), his last discourse to the apostles (Jn 13:31-16:33) and his priestly prayer to the Father (Jn 17). While most striking in St. John's gospel, this unique element of strength and sureness is also found in the synoptics (e.g., Mk 7; Mt 11; Lk 9). And this, I believe, is the point of Guillet's contrast between Jesus' "infallible" discernment and our "groping" discernment. While Jesus' discernment of his identity and mission was really a discernment — obscure, gradual and growing — it was infallible in the sense of unerring.

Infallibility, I find, is a tricky concept. When I ask my students to discuss Jesus' infallible discernment, almost invariably they equate infallibility with clarity. They assume that to be infallible is to have a clear grasp of the situation, to understand fully what God desires and why he desires it. If that is so, then it is indeed difficult to see how the clarity of infallibility could be compatible with the obscurity of discernment. How could something be both perfectly clear and obscure at the same time? It could not. But I don't believe infallibility does, or should, imply clarity of understanding. The great John Courtney Murray, S.J., used to tell us in discussing the Second Vatican Council that it takes about 50 years for the church to grasp fully what a council has defined or declared. The fathers of the council themselves, he said, do not fully understand what they have accomplished. Despite this obscurity, they can speak and act *infallibly*, unerringly, because the Spirit of God guides their deliberations and says through them more than they realize at the time. Similarly, when we affirm that the pope is infallible in certain circumstances, we are not saying that he necessarily has a clear understanding of the matter in question, but rather that he *cannot err* in matters essential to the life of the church. And what is true of pope and council within certain limited areas by reason of their office, is true of the human Jesus in his whole life by reason of his union with the divine Word and his total openness to the Spirit of God at every moment of his life. Like us, he was tempted; unlike us, as Hebrews also says (4:15), he never sinned. He grew as we do, but he never refused growth or said "no" to God, his Father.

Jesus Discerned

Could our discernment, then, also be infallible? Could it be an unerring recognition of *what* God desired of us, even though the *why* was obscure and only gradually made manifest? In theory, yes, *if* we too, like Jesus, were totally open to the Spirit of God. Perhaps the saints do approach this degree of union of wills with the Lord as they mature. But the gospels make clear that even the apostles were not so open during Jesus' public life. They were closed, blocked by self-love, as in the case of the ambitious sons of Zebedee who sought the places of honor in the kingdom of heaven (Mk 10:35-40); or by wealth, as in the case of the rich young man (Mt 19:16-22); or by timidity, as when Peter denied that he knew his Lord in the courtyard of the high priest's house (Lk 22:54-62). In short, the disciples failed in openness. Their attachments — to honor, to wealth, to security, to life itself[5] — complicated and confused their discernment of the person and mission of Jesus.

---

5 Cf. our discussion of these in chapter 5 of *Opening to God,* chapters 3 and 4 of *When the Well Runs Dry* and chapters 1 and 3 of *Darkness in the Marketplace.*

They discerned, but not infallibly or unerringly. Jesus' discernment was unerring because he was totally open to the Spirit. The Holy Spirit could guide him according to the Father's will, even when this will was obscure and unclear to Jesus' human understanding, because he was a man without sin, without disordered attachments. But most of us for most of our lives are like Peter. He loved Jesus; he loved God. But we might say he loved "God and" rather than "God only." He truly wanted God's will. But he wanted other things too. And these other wants, which the saints call disordered attachments when they prevent us from floating free in the sea of God, blocked his discernment of Jesus. This is strikingly illustrated in an incident narrated by both Matthew (16:13-23) and Mark (8:27-33). Jesus asks the disciples, "Who do you say I am?" Peter answers by proclaiming Jesus to be the longed-for Messiah of Israel: "You are the Christ, the Son of the living God." His answer is a great profession of faith in Jesus, and in Matthew's account it leads to Jesus' proclamation that Peter is the rock on which the church will be grounded. Yet, in the very next section, Peter wavers and Jesus calls him "Satan." Why? Because Jesus had gone on to reveal that he was to be a suffering messiah, put to death for the salvation of his people. And Peter was not prepared for this. For centuries the Jewish people had looked forward to the coming of the triumphant messiah, who would liberate the people from colonial oppression. But never did they envision a suffering messiah. Nor could Peter accept such an alien idea. He loved Jesus and firmly believed him to be the Christ, but a Christ conformed to his own ideas, expectations and attachments. How strange—and confusing—it must have seemed to Peter to be praised and blamed virtually in the same breath: praised because he was led by the Spirit of God, and blamed because he was misled by Satan.

Most of us, I believe, identify with Peter as much as anyone in the gospel: his candor, his love, his impetuousness, his very human frailty. It is, moreover, a joy to see Peter grow. In the Acts of the Apostles, when the Spirit of Pentecost has taken possession of him, I think we can perhaps see him move toward a more "infallible" sense of God's word and will in the church. Particularly striking is his part in the controversy concerning the conversion of the gentiles. The vision of the unclean animals which Peter is commanded to eat, contrary to Jewish law, is revealed as a symbol of God's desire that he baptize the pagan household of Cornelius (Acts 10:1-11:18). Peter is troubled and puzzled; he does not understand. But it is "clear" to him that God wills the reception into the faith of this gentile family, especially when the Holy Spirit is poured out upon them in the same way and with the same effects as at Pentecost. There was to be further confusion and hesitation on Peter's part, at least if we listen to St. Paul's account of the dispute (Gal 2:11-14). But at the Council of Jerusalem he unerringly spoke the decisive word in God's name (Acts 15:7-11), and thus the course of the church's development was definitively altered. Never again would it see itself, or be seen by others, as a reform movement of Judaism.

It is important to note that the disciples' discernment concerned the person and mission of Jesus, and not just his doctrine. He himself frequently appealed to his "works" as the basis of belief in him, even when his "words" seemed difficult to grasp (see, e.g., Jn 5:36, 10:25, 10:38). He was their rabbi, their teacher; but his teaching was to be accepted not because of its inherent ethical worth or its logical force, but because it was his, because he proclaimed it. Guillet expresses this beautifully when speaking of the beatitudes pronounced by Jesus:

> After he has chosen his first disciples, his message changes. The kingdom is not only at hand, it is now on the threshold . . . and the division between the good and the bad, awaited by John (the Baptist), is beginning to set men at variance. On the one side are the poor, the unfortunate, the meek, the persecuted; on the other, the rich and the happy. The kingdom with its joy is for the former; misfortune is for the latter.[6]

But this division of men and women into blessed and cursed is not merely "a sort of inventory," a sorting of people "based almost wholly on exterior data." The beatitudes are not a mere mechanical classification, so that all the rich are woeful and all the poor blessed, merely because they happen to be rich or poor. Rather, the blessedness and misery of the rich and the poor de-

---

6 Guillet, *Discernment of Spirits*, p. 34.

pend upon their situation in respect to Jesus himself.

> The beatitudes have meaning only when pronounced by
> Jesus, and they are true only because Jesus is there to
> bring the joy of which he speaks. Otherwise (these
> beatitudes) are only an insult to suffering. The presence
> of Jesus creates the joy of the unfortunate and the riches
> of the poor, and it is this presence that brings about the
> division between the rich and the poor, the happy and
> the persecuted.[7]

The point we are making here is that it is Jesus we discern
and not just his doctrine. The poor are blessed *if* they live in his
presence, and because he declares them to be so. And the rich will
find their riches a burden and a regret, and will feel the need to
be free of this burden, *only if* they have come face to face with
Jesus Christ. Otherwise both the beatitudes and the woes will
seem foolish and romantic. This, I believe, is the difference between Peter and Judas. It is not that Peter found Jesus' teaching
more convincing and clearer than Judas did. In fact, in John
6:68-69, when most of Jesus' hearers and even his disciples have
left him because they found his teaching on the bread of life too
hard to take, Peter answers for the Twelve when Jesus asks if they
too will go away. His reply is: "Lord, whom shall we go to? You
have the message of eternal life, and we believe; we know that
you are the Holy One of God." In effect, Peter chooses not Jesus'
doctrine but Jesus himself. It is as if he said, "Lord, I don't
understand any more than the others. But I trust *you*. Whatever
you say, I accept, because *you* say it." Tragically, Judas never
seems to have found in the person of Jesus what Peter found.
Because he did not, Jesus' teaching never seems to have found a
place in his heart.

Discernment Evaluated

This, of course, is also the challenge for us. We go to the
scripture, not primarily for wise ethical instruction, valuable as
this may be, but to encounter God in the person of Jesus Christ.
The great Mahatma Gandhi found in the gospels the noblest

---

7 *Ibid.*

ethical and moral doctrine in the history of mankind. But he did not have *faith* in Jesus. And so the ongoing debate about the realism and practicality of Gandhi's ideals and methods remains at the level of human reason. For one who, like Peter, encounters a person who is Lord of his life, the question is entirely different. This is evident in the epistles where, as we said earlier, discernment becomes an explicit topic of discussion, especially in the letters of Paul and John. It is now a question of applying the apostolic experience of Jesus to the needs and problems of the early church. Prayer, as the meditative and contemplative "digesting" of the transforming experience of Jesus under the guidance of the Holy Spirit, must now be brought to bear on action, on the concrete situations faced by the apostolic communities. And this meeting point of prayer and action is, as we have indicated, what we mean by discernment.

St. Paul and St. John enumerate several criteria for discernment in the Christian community. Since they form the biblical basis for St. Ignatius' classic rules for discernment, we shall have occasion to refer to them in later chapters. It might be good, though, to conclude this chapter by indicating how these Pauline and Johannine criteria compare with the Old Testament criteria for authentic prophecy which we have discussed in chapter 2. The shifts in emphasis provide an apt summary of what we have seen above concerning the double discernment in the gospels.

When we recall the criteria of authentic prophecy in the Old Testament — misfortune, wondrous signs, fidelity to revealed doctrine, the moral behavior of the prophet, and the inner criteria of his intention and his inaugural vision of Yahweh's choice and mission — the most striking new emphases in John and Paul are their stress on fraternal love and on "one's attitude in relation to Jesus Christ."[8] The common-sense criterion of misfortune — that a prophet proclaiming an unpopular message of bad luck is much less likely to be a fraud — is not found in Paul and John, perhaps because the challenge of a crucified Lord calling his disciples to take up their cross and follow him is already "misfortune" enough! Paul does appeal to the signs of power which he has per-

---

8 Guillet, *op. cit.*, p. 48. He enumerates eight criteria of discernment for St. Paul (pp. 44-48), and seven "laws" from the important First Epistle of John (pp. 51-53).

formed (e.g., 2 Cor 12:12), and both of them appeal to inner experience: Paul's conversion on the Damascus road and John's grounding of his message on what

> we have heard,
> and we have seen with our own eyes;
> that we have watched
> and touched with our hands:
> the Word, who is life (1 Jn 1:1).

The eye of sense sees the human Jesus; the inner eye of love sees, in this bodily experience of the Lord, that "God is light; there is no darkness in him at all" (1:5). As Guillet points out, the true disciple, even one who has not known Jesus in the flesh, has an interior experience of his Spirit (1 Jn 3:24; 4:13) which conveys a "certainty and light independent of any human influence," and this certainty and light fructifies in trust, in an absolute confidence which drives out fear.[9]

As the New Testament stress on fraternal love makes clear, these inner marks of the Spirit of God must bear fruit in signs visible to the Christian community and to all men. He who says he loves God and does not love his neighbor is a liar, "since a man who does not love the brother that he can see cannot love God, whom he has never seen" (1 Jn 4:20; cf., 2:9; 3:10). St. Paul spells out the concrete demands of this criterion of fraternal love in a famous passage in Galatians (5:19-23), a passage which also makes clear that there are diverse and conflicting "spirits" at work in the life of the Christian and his or her community:

> When self-indulgence is at work the results are obvious: fornication, gross indecency and sexual irresponsibility; idolatry and sorcery; feuds and wrangling, jealousy, bad temper and quarrels; disagreements, factions, envy; drunkenness, orgies and similar things. . . . What the Spirit brings is very different: love, joy, peace, patience, kindness, goodness, truthfulness, gentleness and self-control.

Finally, as Guillet points out in discussing the Johannine doctrine on discernment, *all* of these criteria must be verified if the Spirit of God is to be discerned in a concrete situation or choice:

---

9 Guillet, p. 52.

> The centricity of John's perspective gives complete value
> to all the elements within the frame of Christian living:
> confession of faith, authority of the church, concrete
> fidelity to charity, necessity of interior life, communion
> with the Trinity—all these basic principles have equal
> value, all must be accepted unreservedly and developed
> without ulterior motives. Wherever one of them is lack-
> ing, we may be sure that others are lacking also.[10]

It is not enough that only some of the criteria be verified since the
devil, as St. Paul says, enters as an angel of light (2 Cor 11:14). He
can mimic God's voice and appear under the guise of the good
angel. But if all the signs are good, we can trust the inspiration to
act or decide as coming from the Spirit of God. As we shall see in
part III, even when there are apparently good fruits the "tail of
the snake" will always give away the action of the evil spirit, at
least for those who have matured in discerning love.

Conclusion

Thus we have seen in this chapter that the New Testament
does present us with a solid and comprehensive picture of discernment in Christian life. It is based upon a concept of God as the
Father of mature sons and daughters, and it finds its model and
its focus in a human Jesus who himself lived a life of discerning
love and became for us the object of our own discernment.
Moreover, we "discern Jesus" not merely in prayer but in the concrete situations of our life as a Christian community. Finally, in
exploring the idea of discernment in the Old and New
Testaments, we have sought to understand more clearly what
precisely discernment means, and what kind of people we would
have to be to discern Jesus and his Father's will in our lives today.
Before turning to the classic Ignatian rules for discernment, let
us, then, in the next chapter, summarize and make concrete the
prerequisites for discerning love which we have discovered in the
scriptures.

---

10 *Ibid.* p. 53.

Practicum Questions

1. Would the discussion whether Jesus truly discerned his own person and mission, and if so whether he discerned "infallibly," be of any *practical* relevance to your own life of discernment?

2. John the Baptist is one of the great transitional figures, from the old covenant to the new. In his person the whole Old Testament seeks, as it were, to discern in Jesus the promised Messiah. If you could meet John, what would you like to ask him about his discernment of Jesus and/or of his own mission and identity? (For your convenience, the following are the principal gospel passages referring to John the Baptist: John 1:6, 15, 19-36; 3:25-30; 5:33-36; 10:41; and Matthew—with appropriate parallel passages in Mark and Luke—3:1-17; 4:12; 9:14 ff.; 11:2-19; 14:1-12; 16:14; 17:13; 21:25-27.)

Chapter 3
The Climate of Our Discernment

As our discussion of the New Testament revelation has made clear, the art of discernment is an essential gift for the life of the church. At the same time, however, it is a relatively uncommon art. In recent years much has been written about it, and the word is heard frequently in religious circles; yet how rare genuine discernment is. Even when people understand the difference between spiritual discernment and decision making (and often they do not), they still find it extremely difficult to know how to discern authentically and fruitfully. The problem, I believe, is not that the principles of discernment itself are difficult or obscure, but rather that the *climate* of discernment — the dispositions of soul necessary before one can even begin to discern — is one of total commitment to the Lord. This implies a "blank check" attitude toward his will in our life, an attitude such as Jesus himself had in relation to the Father.

The criteria of authentic prophecy which we have seen, or the New Testament norms for discernment given by Paul and John, are not always easy to apply in practice. But they are relatively clear, especially when we see them exemplified in the life of the early church and of Jesus himself. What is more problematic is the fundamental disposition of soul presupposed for the use of these criteria. That is, the real problem in choosing the right neckties for another person is not so much knowing the various possible types and styles of neckties but knowing, with the knowledge born of love, the *person himself.* What kind of person is he? And what kind of person must I be — what kind of relationship must there be between us — if I am to know him and his tastes and desires? It is this latter question to which I refer in speaking of the "climate" of discernment.

We have seen this climate operative in Jesus' life and, to a lesser degree ("gropingly," because of their attachments), in the lives of Peter and the other disciples. One principal value of beginning our study with the scripture is that it helps us to clarify the Christian meaning of discernment. Now, however, we need to apply this biblical vision to our own lives as 20th-century women and men. In this chapter we ask about the climate of discernment in our lives today.

Since discernment deals with concrete decisions and specific situations which call for an active response, let us begin by imagining three typical discerning situations — situations in which troubled souls might seek out a spiritual director to help them determine God's will for themselves.

Three Cases for Discernment

Joe is a theologian in a diocesan seminary, and the eldest son of a large and poor family which seems to need his help. Letitia is a newly professed sister in an active religious community, a community experiencing serious tensions concerning the degree and kind of sociopolitical involvement proper to their vowed life. Maria and Ed's marriage has begun to disintegrate: It seems that they are simply incompatible, and yet they have four young children to think of. Each of them — Maria and Ed, Letty and Joe — is caught up in a painful, though all too common, human dilemma. To be human, in fact, is to encounter such crisis moments, when there seems to be no clearly correct course of action. Should Joe remain in the seminary and pursue the vocation to which he feels strongly called? Or is he simply escaping his primary responsibility to his family: living a secure life with many opportunities and advantages while they are suffering? And Letty, what is her responsibility to engage herself in the present struggle for social and political justice? Her community is badly divided on the question. Some argue that such involvement is alien to the evangelical lifestyle of a religious, while others argue, equally forcefully, that the gospel demands such involvement of a true follower of Christ today. To complicate matters further, both groups quote statements of the Holy Father and the church to support their opposing views. What should Letty think? What should she do?

Though Maria and Ed are not religious or seminarians, let us assume (as is already implicit in the cases of Letty and Joe) that they are committed Christians who sincerely wish to find the gospel solution to their dilemma. At least one good priest has already implied that there is a solid chance that their marriage could be annulled by the church (perhaps because of their state of mind at the time of the marriage). At the very least, permission for a legal separation could easily be obtained. But what about the children? For better or worse, the children exist and are their responsibility. Can they best fulfill that responsibility by separating (so that the children could at least grow up in a peaceful environment) or by remaining together (so that the children would know the presence and influence of a father during their critical formative years)? Which is better? Maria and Ed have been flooded with advice, and even pressure, from family and friends. But what does God want?

The "Discerning" Dimension

As we said earlier, such dilemmas are, unfortunately, a normal part of our life on this earth. Sometimes the crisis is big; sometimes it is relatively small. But we all encounter situations, problems which seem to admit of no simple, clearly correct solution. For the unbeliever — or for the "believer" whose faith plays a negligible part in the living of his life — the choice will have to depend on reason (weighing the pros and cons for each alternative), or on intuition (which is often a polite name for emotion and our instinctual attachments). But for the committed believer, such as we have assumed Maria and Ed and Letty and Joe to be, the question "What should I do?" becomes "What is God's will for me in this crisis situation? What does the Lord really want?" Though our troubled friends may never have heard the word, this is really the question of *discernment*.

As a preliminary description we can say that discernment is the art of finding God's will in the concrete life situations which confront us. What does the Lord really want of Ed and Maria? Of Joe? Of Letty? Sometimes his will is quite clear — for example, that a mother should give her young children their breakfast on an ordinary day — and the "discernment" involved is so automatic that we do not even advert to it. In such cases we could perhaps still speak of discernment, in the sense of a habitual, spontaneous sensitivity to what pleases the Lord. But normally the word refers to situations such as we have described, where there is ambiguity, that is, where it is unclear what God really wants.

Presuppositions of Discernment

In such ambiguous situations, one needs to discern if he or she is to discover how the Lord is speaking in and through the crisis situation. But in order to do so, it is necessary that the discerner be possessed of certain qualities or predispositions. We may enumerate three which are crucial:

(1) A desire to do God's will. In the first place, discernment presupposes a committed faith in the Lord. We mentioned this earlier, but now we need to spell out in more detail the *kind* of commitment required if we are to be discerning persons. We have already said that by the words "committed believer" we mean a person who sincerely desires to do God's will, to accomplish his work in this concrete given world. Unless it really makes a difference to me what he desires — unless I truly want, or at least desire to want, what he wants — discernment will be impossible. This is the first presupposition of any genuine discernment. And it is a demanding one: We can hardly speak of discernment in the life of a person for whom God is unimportant or even minimally important. We have already assumed much in postulating that Joe, Letty, Ed and Maria are persons who really care about God's will in their lives.

Our classic source on discernment is the *Spiritual Exercises* of St. Ignatius Loyola, a guidebook for the retreatant and the director in a 30-day retreat. The *Spiritual Exercises*, written in the 16th century, have become the inspired paradigm for all the various retreat traditions which have enriched the church since that time — and St. Ignatius the patron saint of retreats and retreat directors. Ignatius does not discuss much this first presupposition of ours, the reason being that he assumes this disposition as given in any proper candidate for a retreat. He takes it for granted that the retreatant is so disposed; if not, he says,

> it is more suitable to give him some of the easier exercises as a preparation for confession. Then he should be given some ways of examining his conscience, and directed to confess more frequently than was his custom before, so as to retain what he has gained. But let him not go on any further and take up the matter dealing with the choice of a way of life,[1]

which will be the context for Ignatius' introduction of the topic of discernment. If people do not have a sincere and operative desire to do God's will in their lives, it is better to lay the groundwork now, to seek to dispose them, with the hope that at some future time they will be able to make a truly fruitful discerning retreat. That desire to do God's will which we have called a "committed faith" is the first essential prerequisite for genuine discernment.

(2) Openness to God. But it is not sufficient that the discerning person be "pious" or devout. God may play a significant role in a person's life, and yet there may be no genuine desire to do his will. In fact, one may be a religious fanatic — obsessed by God, by the glory of God — and merely be wedded to one's own idea of God and God's will. This, of course, is not really desiring the Lord's will. But it is a very dangerous and deceptive counterfeit, which has caused much suffering in the history of religion and in the lives of individuals. To genuinely desire God's will, one must be truly *open* to God, a God who is always mysterious and often surprising and disturbing, as Kierkegaard so passionately insisted.

All of us — even the best of us — will find that our ideas of God frequently block us from truly experiencing him as he reveals himself. This, it seems to me, was the problem of the Pharisees: They could not properly discern the person and mission of Jesus, and his call to them, because they were blinded by their own preconceptions, their own attachments. They were religious zealots but, perhaps without realizing it, they sought "God and" their own ideas rather than "God only." But even the apostles, on Ascension day, were still asking: "Lord. . . . are you going to restore the kingdom to Israel?" (Acts 1:6). They had been with

---

1 *The Spiritual Exercises of St. Ignatius*, translated by Louis J. Puhl, S.J. (Newman Press, 1960), #18. There are many good recent translations of the *Spiritual Exercises*; most of them use the same paragraph numbering as Puhl, so we will refer here to paragraphs (e.g., #18) instead of page numbers.

him all those years, listening to his teaching and marveling at his miracles, and they still did not understand him. Their own Jewish ideas of messianism and kingship still filled their minds and blocked their understanding. Real openness is a Pentecost gift, in our lives as well as in theirs. We must pray for it, and the Spirit must give it. Unless we are truly open to the Lord, we cannot discern. No wonder the mature pray-er finds the prayer of the possessed boy's father coming more and more to her own lips: "I do have faith. Help the little faith I have!" (Mk 9:25).

St. Ignatius discusses this openness to God in his "Introduction to Making a Choice of a Way of Life" (#169). This comes at the end of the second week of the *Spiritual Exercises*. The retreatant has come to an honest, Spirit-guided knowledge of himself or herself — to a vision of self as seen by God — in the first week. In the second week, he or she has turned from self-knowledge to a contemplation of Jesus Christ in his public life on earth. Having come "naked" before the Lord in the first week, the retreatant now seeks to put on the Lord Jesus, to be filled with Christ. For St. Ignatius, always the man of action and service, this means discovering God's will for us. As he says (#1): "We call spiritual exercises every way of preparing and disposing the soul to rid itself of all inordinate attachments, and, after their removal, of seeking and finding the will of God in the disposition of our life for the salvation of our soul."

In his introduction to choosing a way of life (#169), he summarizes the process of detachment through which the soul has journeyed in the preceding two weeks. If the retreat has been fruitful, then the retreatant should find in these words a confirmation of his or her own present disposition: "In every good choice, so far as depends on us, our intention must be simple. I must consider only the end for which I am created, that is, for the praise of God our Lord and for the salvation of my soul. Hence, whatever I choose must help me to this end for which I am created." This simplicity of intention, which we have called genuine openness to God, is easy to describe but difficult to realize in practice.

Ignatius puts the problem in terms of means and ends: "I must not subject and fit the end to the means, but the means to the end. Many first choose marriage, which is a means, and secondarily the service of God our Lord in marriage, though the service of God is the end." As I have discovered in quoting this passage in talks to married people, Ignatius' words are as true today as they were 400 years ago when he wrote them. Good souls have God as their end, they sincerely desire to serve and love him. But it is much more difficult to have him as my *only* end. In fact, most of us are married (or ordained) long before we come to realize that we have made ends of means, that we have chosen "God and" rather than "God only." Fortunately the Lord is patient and understanding, and does write straight with our crooked lines. The fact remains, however, that our capacity to discern is directly proportioned to our openness to God, our simplicity of intention.

(3) A knowledge of God. There is one further presupposition for genuine discernment. One might desire to do God's will but have no idea how to discover it. He or she might have good desires but no solid knowledge of God and his ways. In such a case, too, discernment would be impossible. A committed faith must also be an enlightened faith, a faith based on solid experiential knowledge of the person to whom I commit myself. If I don't know you, I can scarcely know what pleases you.

There is a story which I've told before[2] which may make this clear. One day when I was visiting my family in the U.S. I went shopping with my mother. She wanted to buy a necktie for my father for Father's Day. As she surveyed a whole table covered with neckties for sale, she quickly selected four or five that he would like and then, inspecting those few more closely, chose the one or two which would please him most. And she was right! He did like the neckties she chose. It was evident to me that she *knew* what he would really like. How? Only because she had shared his life for 40 years, because she had that love-born "knowledge by connaturality" of which we spoke in chapter 2. Much as I loved my father, I could never have chosen so unerringly what would really please him. I had been away from home, in the seminary and in the Philippines, for many years. My experience of my

---

2 See *Opening to God*, ch. 3, p. 43.

father—my experiential knowledge of him—was much less than hers.

So discernment of God's will depends upon our lived experience, our experiential knowledge of him. And my little story about the neckties brings out another important point about discernment: The less personal experience I have of the Lord, the more I will have to depend on someone else, who has this lived experience, to teach me what pleases him. This is the meaning of "spiritual direction" in the Christian tradition. The director, ideally, is someone who has longer and deeper experience of the Lord than I have. Hence he or she can help me to determine what pleases him. If I wanted to buy my father a necktie, it would be wise to bring my mother shopping with me, and to seek her advice in my choice, at least if I wanted to choose what he would like and not what I think he should like. It is the same with God. The spiritual director does not choose for me; it is my gift to the Lord which is in question here, and so the choice must be mine. But the director, like my mother, can be a very good interpreter—a co-discerner, to use the name I prefer—in guiding me to a choice which will really please the One I desire to please. That is why Joe, Letty, Ed and Maria seek direction in their several dilemmas. They want to do God's will. They want to please him, but they find themselves unsure about what he really wants. So they come to someone whom they believe to be more experienced in God's ways; someone who can help them to discern what is really the Lord's will in these concrete, obscure situations. For this reason, I would say that the normal (though not essential) *context* of discernment is spiritual direction, especially for beginners in the spiritual life. In fact, I begin and end my course on discernment with a discussion of spiritual direction.

What we have just said, however, implies that direction, co-discernment, would be less necessary as we ourselves become more experienced in the ways of the Lord. This is true, which is why I like to see the spiritual director as a *co*-discerner. The primary discerner is the directee. The role of the director is not to make the directee perpetually dependent on himself or herself, but to bring the directee to that personal experience of the Lord which will enable one to make personal discerning judgments about the will of God in his or her life. However, I do believe that spiritual direction is desirable as long as one lives, at least if one wishes to grow in sensitivity to what pleases the Lord. As we shall explain more fully later, this is because our commitment to the Lord, unlike my choice of a necktie for my father, involves the surrender of my whole being. And "the world, the flesh and the devil" will be working until my dying breath to prevent this surrender and to confuse my choice. Nonetheless, despite the lifelong value of direction, it remains true that the primary role of the director is to help one come to maturity of spirit: to bring the soul to an ever-deeper knowledge of, and an ever-greater sensitivity to, the Spirit of God.

More Difficult Than Choosing Neckties

Thus we have seen three presuppositions of genuine discernment in the life of the Christian. It might be helpful to summarize them before we proceed further:

(1) Discernment presupposes a person who truly desires to accomplish God's work in the concrete, confused situations of life. That is, it matters to such a person what the Lord wants.

(2) Discernment further presupposes a person who is truly open to be taught by, and led by, the Lord. This is implied in (1), but I believe it is important to make it explicit, since many of us "work for God" (choose for him the necktie which we like and which we want him to like) rather than being truly open to "do God's work" (choose for him the necktie which he desires). We do desire to work for him—he is important to us—but we never learn to let him be the boss.

(3) Finally, in order for the first two presuppositions to be fruitful, the discerner must "know" the Lord in the biblical sense of an experiential knowledge born of love.[3] If one lacks this per-

---

3 See John L. McKenzie, *Dictionary of the Bible* (Milwaukee, Bruce, 1965), the entry for the word "know": "The Israelite knew with the heart, and Hebrew has no word which corresponds exactly to our 'mind' or 'intellect.' The distinction between intellect and appetite is therefore imprecise. In general it may be said that in Hebrew to know is to experience; experience develops into acceptance or possession" (p. 485). McKenzie then gives numerous examples of this biblical sense of "know," which corresponds to what we called earlier the "connaturality of love."

sonal experience of God, then it will be necessary to seek the help of a co-discerner, a director who does know the Lord. In the immediate crisis the director can interpret for me what the Lord desires, but his or her primary role is to guide me to that personal knowledge which will enable me to become a discerning person myself.

Joe and Letty are young. Thus they will probably have little experience of God, and much greater need to depend on the discerning help of their directors. When Joe is Father Joe, celebrating his golden jubilee in the priesthood, he himself, please God, will be much more knowledgeable in the ways of the Lord. He will be much more capable of discerning for himself. But whether I depend much on a more experienced director or have gradually become a discerning lover myself, the essence of discernment is the same. It is the meeting point of prayer and action, where prayer is understood as the love relationship between the soul and God. St. Ignatius calls it *discreta caritas*, discerning love, which captures beautifully the essential truth that discernment is a function of a loving, personal relationship to the Lord. It can normally be only as deep and as solid as that relationship itself. The true discerner must be a praying, loving person.

In this sense, discerning love and choosing neckties are similar. Discernment is the fruit of a long "living with" the Lord, just as my mother's sense of what necktie would please my father depended upon the deep sharing of their lives over the 42 years they lived together. In both cases, it is only continual and loving contact with the beloved which can give us such sensitivity. People who have lived long together in love can read between the lines; they are responsive to the smallest sign of what pleases or displeases the one they love. They can read in the eyes what has not been said in words.

It is at this point, however, that our necktie analogy seems to break down when applied to God. We don't see him the way a wife sees her husband. We don't hear his voice with our ears. Or if we think we do hear it, we can never have the same certainty that it is really his voice as a wife can have about her husband's voice.

The problem is not merely that God is spirit and has no eyes or voice in our human sense. This problem could be overcome by our faith that he does speak to us sacramentally and bodily, with the voice of the prophet, the priest, the pope, the scriptural authors. But the real problem in hearing the voice of God is that, as scripture itself tells us and as we have explained in the previous chapters, there are many counterfeit voices competing with God's voice. Jesus himself says that there will be false prophets (Mt 7:15), and John speaks of the world, the flesh and the devil as subtle adversaries against whom we must always be on our guard (cf. 1 Jn 2:15-17 and 5:18-19). Since these competing voices will all claim to be God's voice, even the good will be deceived unless they

> put God's armor on so as to be able to resist the devil's tactics. For it is not against human enemies that we have to struggle, but against the Sovereignties and the Powers who originate the darkness in this world, the spiritual army of evil in the heavens. That is why you must rely on God's armor, or you will not be able to put up any resistance when the worst happens (Eph 6:11-13).

When Paul is defending himself against his adversaries in the Corinthian church he says:

> These people are counterfeit apostles, they are dishonest workmen disguised as apostles of Christ. There is nothing unexpected about that; if Satan himself goes disguised as an angel of light, there is no need to be surprised when his servants, too, disguise themselves as the servants of righteousness (2 Cor 11:13-15).

This is a second reason (in addition to the mature, loving knowledge of the Lord which is required) why discernment is not easy; the devil appears as an "angel of light." He is willing to join the church choir and sing the praises of God, if only he can bring the choir members to his kingdom in the end. He is willing to promote social justice, to defend the divine authority of the hierarchy, to sponsor charismatic prayer groups, as long as the end result is not the kingdom of God but the destruction of that kingdom. This is true even for those who are deeply committed to God. No matter how deep our loving knowledge of the Lord, in this life we always live by dark faith and not by clear vision.

In this connection, it is striking that St. Ignatius Loyola, one of the church's pre-eminent masters of discernment, prefaces his Rules for Discernment with these words: "Rules for perceiving and understanding *to some degree* the different movements that are produced in the soul — the good, that they may be accepted; the bad, that they may be rejected."[4] Our discernment is always "to some degree" only; it is tentative and reformable because it is made in faith, and because it relates to concrete decisions in situations where the evidence is conflicting or ambivalent. Discernment is not a way of short-circuiting faith; rather, it is a way of choosing how to act in faith.

The Essential Qualities of Heart of the Discerner

Given the ambivalence and open-endedness of the discerning situation, and given the experiential knowledge of an invisible Lover on which discernment depends, certain qualities will be necessary if one is to be a truly discerning person. Such a person must always be humble, charitable and courageous. He or she must be *humble*, because faith situations are obscure, and because our discernment is always impeded to some extent by our own sinfulness. St. John of the Cross has said that one of the surest signs of interior growth is a growing awareness of our own sinfulness. If we transpose this to the domain of apostolic decision making, the genuinely discerning soul should always be marked by a healthy self-doubt and by an openness to be guided by the Lord through others. This is why obedience played such a large part in medieval discussions of discernment. Even today, when we lay more stress on the personal maturity and responsibility of the directee, that docility which is born of humility is still a crucial sign of genuine discernment.

Moreover, the true discerner must be *charitable*, since as a mature pray-er, such a person knows well his or her own

---

4 *The Spiritual Exercises of St. Ignatius*, #313, emphasis added. This is the preface to the rules for the first week of the *Spiritual Exercises*. The rules for the second week provide a "more accurate discernment" (#328), because they presuppose a deeper experiential knowledge of God. But, as the rules themselves make clear, the "evil spirit" also becomes more subtle in his tactics as we mature. In fact, John of the Cross says that the devil will work far more to deceive one committed and deep soul — especially one who can influence the lives of others — than to inflict harm on numerous less-committed souls (*Living Flame of Love*, Stanza III, #64).

weakness and sinfulness and capacity for self-deception. Thus he or she will be very slow to judge others harshly because they happen to see things differently. Even if my discernment is genuine, what I discern is the Lord's will *for me* here and now (or *for us*, in the far more complex case of communal discernment, which demands consensus on the part of the group discerning). I do not usually discern for someone else, unless the Lord has made me a prophet, a co-discerner, in their lives. Even Peter, whom the Lord made the foundation stone of the church, could not inquire into Jesus' plans for John. When he tried to do so, Jesus rebuked him: "If I want him to stay behind until I come, what does it matter to you? You are to follow me" (Jn 21:22). If even the first pope could not inquire into the Lord's designs for others, how can I sit in judgment on them?

Despite the humility and charity of a wise discerner, such a person must also be *courageous.* That is, the healthy self-doubt in the genuine discerner's heart does not lead to timidity or paralysis, but rather to the courage to risk. Actually, the discerner does have a certain "certitude" concerning the Lord's will for him or her. It is a certitude of faith and not of reason; and it is a practical certitude rather than theoretical; that is, I feel sure, after prayer and openness to direction, that I should act in this way here and now, and I am convinced that such action is the only honest, loving thing for me to do. I may not know the reasons why. Objectively, I may be mistaken. But the Lord does not ask us, thank God!, to be always right. What he asks is that we be always honest, always true to the best understanding of his will that we can attain to. Kierkegaard captured the enormous difference between being right and being honest when he defined religious truth as "an objective uncertainty held fast in an appropriation process of the most passionate inwardness." That is, there is subjective (even "passionate") conviction, after I have properly discerned, that this course of action is truly God's will for me. But usually there is also "objective uncertainty," no clear understanding of why the Lord wills this.[5] At times our discern-

_____

5 Surprisingly, perhaps, this "objective uncertainty" will increase rather than diminish as our prayer life matures. As we are drawn to live more and more totally in the dark night (or dry well or cloud of unknowing) of faith, there is less and less

ment in faith will even do violence to our understanding of what would be best. A classic instance of this, beloved of Kierkegaard, is Abraham's call to slay Isaac, his only son, despite Yahweh's promise that he was to be the father of "a great nation" (Gn 18:18). To embrace such a call, once discerned, with passionate inwardness will surely require great courage.

Letty's Dilemma

We began our discussion of the context of discernment with Joe, Letty, Ed and Maria; their concrete problems provided the occasion for our discussion of the nature and the context of discernment. Each of them was confronted with a personal crisis, which he or she saw not merely as a problem calling for a human solution but as a challenge to discover and follow God's will in their lives; and each came to a spiritual director for help in discerning the Lord's solution to their dilemma. Now, as a clarification and practical test of all we have seen and said, let us return to them — specifically to Letty — to see what it would mean to handle her problem in a discerning spirit.

You recall Letty's dilemma. She is newly professed as a member of an apostolic religious community. Her congregation, like so many others today, is confronted with the need, in the spirit of Vatican II and of the teaching of recent popes, to witness to faith *and* to promote social justice. Gone are the days when the active religious could rest comfortably in a clear distinction between sacred and secular roles, in a vision of religious life as witnessing to faith alone, while the task of promoting social justice is left to the laity. More and more clearly faith and justice, whether in the first world context of minority rights and nuclear warfare or in the third world context of liberation and development, are seen as inseparable. The religious and the "secular," the eschatological and the incarnational dimensions of Christian faith are both integral parts of a single proclamation of the gospel.

---

understanding of how the Lord is working (cf. St. John of the Cross, *The Ascent of Mount Carmel*, II, 6, #2). The point of my book, *Darkness in the Marketplace*, is that this darkness will occur in our active (marketplace) lives as well as in our prayer lives.

In theory this integral vocation is clear. But in practice it has resulted in serious tensions for the apostles of our day. How does a congregation achieve the integration of both ends in a single ministry? How does an individual realize in his or her one small life the twofold call to witness to faith and to promote social justice? There are only 24 hours in the day. It seems clear that no one of us — and no single group of us either — can do the whole job. Thus it is that tensions arise, as we try to discern what part of the total Christian mission is really entrusted to us personally.

Letty's community, as we saw it, is divided on the question. One group feels that a religious is, by definition, primarily a witness to faith, and that the task of promoting social justice is primarily a function of the lay Christian, particularly insofar as it entails "activism" and political involvement. The other group feels that this distinction between lay and religious functions is unreal and unrealistic in the present situation. For them, any proclamation of the gospel that does not center on the question of social injustice, and on the need for "liberation" from human oppression of person by person, is at best irrelevant and at worst cowardly. To complicate matters further, both groups can (and do) quote scripture and recent church documents in support of their opposing views.

What can we tell Letty? The first thing we should say, I believe, is that such disagreements and divergences of opinion are inevitable in our life of faith. They begin in the earliest days of the church, with the confrontation of Peter and Paul and James concerning the judaizing of the gentile converts. If all questions yielded clear-cut rational solutions, there would be no need for faith, and no need for discernment. Far from being discouraged by the uncertainty she feels, Letty should see it as a normal call to a deeper faith and trust in the Lord, as well as a call to grow in sensitivity to his way of speaking.

To become more sensitive to his voice, Letty will have to realize that the Lord always speaks *in peace*. Turmoil, anxiety and restlessness are never signs of his voice for her, since they are forms of desolation. This is the most basic of the rules for discernment proper, which we shall discuss in the chapters to follow and which is already implicit in what we said about the humility and charity which are essential qualities of a truly discerning person. The courage of the soul truly open to the Lord is never marked by angry self-righteousness or restless intolerance.

If the two groups in Letty's community are busy excommunicating each other — if their disagreement is not marked by loyalty and love and an openness to the faith vision of others — then Letty is faced with a very difficult situation indeed. The Spirit of God is scarcely at work in a community at war within itself. Let us assume, however, that the climate of the congregation is loving and humble and courageous, although they are still divided on what God is really asking of them as religious today.[6]

In that case, we can turn to Letty and her personal dilemma. We could begin by inquiring about her own openness to God's will and her knowledge of his ways. The latter is presumably slight since Letty is young and new to a life of prayer. But what about her humility and charity and courage, as we have described these qualities earlier? Is she truly open to learn and to grow? The very fact she has come for direction is a promising sign of her docility. Is she loyal to the congregation, pained by the division she sees, and desirous of being a healer and unifier insofar as this is possible? This is a lot to ask of one who has just finished her novitiate. But such loyalty is not rare in young religious today, thank God. And, if present, it provides hope of a solid and lasting vocation, as well as a capacity to discern authentically in the present crisis. If Letty is this type of person, her charity and humility and courage are solid.

The Letty we describe would also possess the first two presuppositions of discernment as discussed at the beginning of this chapter: a desire to find God's will, and a sincere openness to "do God's work" and not merely to "work for God." It would be good though to explain the latter point to her. Frequently the distinction between doing God's work (what he wants) and work-

---

6 We could also, of course, help Letty to discern her calling even in a bad community situation. The guidelines for her own personal discernment would be essentially the same. But the problem would be much more difficult and painful, particularly for a newly professed religious like Letty. She has not yet come to a mature personal relationship to the Lord, and is thus much more dependent on the concrete vision and values of the congregation.

ing for God (what I want for him)[7] is not clear even to mature religious. And I would guess, from my own experience as a director and as a religious, that fully grasping the distinction implies a rather advanced and somewhat rare spirituality.

If Letty has not yet discovered the real meaning of doing God's work—or does not possess one or more of the other prerequisites discussed above—a good director should be prepared to assist her in the slow process of acquiring a discerning heart. This will take time and patience. It would be much easier just to give Letty an answer to her immediate problem. It would be quicker to give her *my* opinion on the activism-evangelization problem, and my reasons for feeling that she should follow my opinion. This is the quick way and thus the usual way, but it is not the discerning way. After such "direction" Letty will be no closer to possessing the *discreta caritas* of which we speak. And when she becomes old Sister Letty, full of years and experience but not of discernment, she will still not know how to determine what kind of neckties please the Lord she loves.

Thus Letty—and Joe and Ed and Maria, since they too are young in the ways of the Lord—will probably have to depend much on a good director in discovering God's will for herself. The third presupposition of discernment, a deep experiential knowledge of the Lord and of what pleases him, usually is realized only slowly and after many years of living with the Lord. Even in this early stage of Letty's life, however, the director should be non-directive, a co-discerner. He should assist her to discover *in her own experience* the signs of what pleases the Lord. He should teach her to discern God's voice from the other competing voices by helping her discover what to look for within herself. If the director does his work well, and if Letty is truly open to guidance and growth, then the specific dilemma which led her to seek direction will become the occasion for a much broader maturing in the Lord. She will indeed discover God's will for her in this concrete situation. But she will also discover much more: She will learn to read the "signs of the times" in her own life and in the life of her community. She will learn how to

---

7 For an exploration of this distinction see chapters 2 and 3 of *Darkness in the Marketplace*.

discover the will of God in all the crossroads situations which will confront her in the long years ahead. She will become, by the grace of God, a truly discerning person.

Signs of the Times

What are those "signs" of God's time which a good director can teach Letty to discern? They are the rules for discernment, which have been given classic formulation in the *Spiritual Exercises* of St. Ignatius Loyola.[8] The present chapter has been concerned with the context or "climate" of discernment in spiritual direction and not with the actual process of discernment itself. That is, we have been concerned with the conditions and prerequisites for genuine discernment. The actual process of discerning will be the subject of parts II and III. We have already noted, however, that the basic criteria for all discernment are found in scripture, in passages such as Galatians 5:22-23 ("What the spirit brings is very different: love, joy, peace, patience, kindness, goodness, trustfulness, gentleness and self-control"); 1 John 4:2 ("You can tell the spirits that come from God by this: every spirit which acknowledges that Jesus the Christ has come in the flesh is from God"); John 13:35 ("By this love you have for one another, everyone will know that you are my disciples") and 14:27 ("Peace I bequeath to you; my own peace I give you"). These are some of the fruits of the Spirit of God, by which we judge his presence and action in us.

And what of the fruits of the evil spirit, who is also always at work in our lives? They will either be the opposite of the fruits of the good spirit (turmoil instead of peace), or they will counterfeit the fruits of the good spirit (a love of family or country which appears good but is really disordered, and ultimately is not love at all). Since the devil often comes as an angel of light, it is not always easy to determine whether the fruits that appear are gen-

---

8 *The Spiritual Exercises of St. Ignatius*, #313-336. In the popular Image Book translation of Anthony Mottola, in which the paragraphs are not numbered, the rules are on pages 129-134. On the topic of spiritual direction, as the ordinary context of discernment for beginners, see the excellent monograph, "Contemporary Spiritual Direction: Scope and Principles" by William J. Connolly, S.J., which is volume VII, number 3 (1975) in the series, *Studies in the Spirituality of Jesuits*.

uine signs of the good spirit. Communities that gather to pray in the name of Christ, or to work for his glory, may really be led by self-seeking and marked by an intolerance which easily masquerades as generosity and holy zeal. But if Letty perseveres and becomes a discerning person, she will gradually learn to sense and judge these fruits, good and bad, in her own life and prayer.

What, then, is the answer to the concrete problem with which we began our discussion? Should Letty opt for activism or for non-involvement? We have not said in this chapter, because we cannot say. Only the Lord can answer the question, since it is his will that we seek. Sometimes obedience, the charism of the congregation, or other circumstantial factors will make his will clear. Often enough, however, there will still be ambiguity even after all these factors have been considered. Then Sister Letty—or seminarian Joe[9] or Ed and Maria—must turn within to prayer and read the signs of the diverse spirits at work in their lives. Usually they will need a guide, a co-discerner, to help them in this task of discerning love: someone with more experience than they in the ways of the Lord, and someone willing to journey with them to that point of discernment where prayer meets action. What we have shown, I trust, is the *kind* of persons Letty and her director must be if their journey is to be fruitful. But if she is well started on the road of discerning love, then it may not be of prime importance to Letty what specific work she is doing, as long as it is God's work.

Practicum Question

Describe a significant discernment situation in your own life experience (cf., the situations of Joe, Letty, Ed and Maria described in this chapter). What was the precise point to be discerned in your situation? Also, considering the three prerequisites and three related essential qualities of heart mentioned in the chapter, how well disposed were you for genuine and fruitful discernment?

---

9 Whose case was discussed in *Opening to God*, pp. 51-52.

Part II
Sowing the Good Seed

Chapter 4
Good Times for a Good Choice

In the earlier chapters of this book we spoke of "preparing the soil" (as the first part was entitled) for a fruitful harvest of discernment. Basically, we have considered two essential dimensions of this preparation: a clarification of the meaning of the term "discernment," with the help of the Old and New Testaments; and a discussion of the dispositions of soul—what we have called "prerequisites" and "essential qualities of heart"—necessary if one is to be a truly discerning person. The first dimension, a clear grasp of what discernment is, is essential if our practice of discernment is to be grounded on a solid and correct understanding of God's ways with his people, with us. The God of Jesus Christ, as we have seen, chooses to relate to us as a loving Father to adult children. He desires that we be mature and responsible partners in the work of continuing creation and redemption. At the same time, his is not the only "voice" which men and women hear; there are conflicting voices competing for our attention. Later in the book we shall have to explore the nature and origin of these voices, and we shall see that they differ—or speak with different accents—at various stages of our maturing.

The second essential dimension of our preparing of the soil was our discussion of the prerequisites for sound discernment and the qualities of heart essential for discerning love. The third prerequisite we saw is a knowledge of God's ways; and we noted that this is not a common quality, especially among beginners. For this reason, a good director or "co-discerner" is often needed. The problem, however, is that good direction and good directors are rare. Moreover, the role of a good director, even when one is to be found, is not to make people dependent on himself or herself, but to help them to become mature, discerning pray-ers themselves. For both of these reasons, it is important that we be able to make available to as many committed Christians as possible the tools whereby they can live a life of discerning love.

In the past several years, my course on discernment has attracted an overflow enrollment, with the students about equally divided among priests (or seminarians), sisters and laypersons. The presence of the laity, and the great profit they have derived from the course, has been a special joy to me. Despite their initial sense of inadequacy in sharing with sisters, seminarians and priests, they soon discover that they have much to give—that, in fact, they bring to discernment a unique wealth of experience which is a valuable complement of that of the religious and priests. They have various reasons for taking the course: Some are with charismatic groups, others are involved in parish-based apostolates, and a few are seeking to apply discernment at a crucial moment in their own Christian lives. Whatever their reasons for attending the course, the profit they derive from it has convinced me that the art of discernment should be shared with a much wider segment of the Christian community.

There is a beautiful passage in Exodus (18:13-27), which gives concrete embodiment to what I have discovered. Found in the office of readings for Thursday of the second week of Lent, it tells of Moses' work as a judge in the Israelite community. His father-in-law sees him at this labor "from morning till evening," and asks him what he is doing and why. Moses replies: "Because the people come to me to bring their enquiries to God. When they have some dispute they come to me, and I settle the differences between the one and the other and I instruct them in God's statutes and his decisions." His father-in-law objects that the burden Moses carries is too heavy for one man, that "you will tire yourself out, you and the people with you." He suggests that Moses share and divide the labor of judgment in Israel:

> You ought to represent the people before God and bring
> their disputes to him. Teach them the statutes and the
> decisions; show them the way they must follow and what
> their course must be. But choose from the people at large
> some capable and God-fearing men, trustworthy and in-
> corruptible, and appoint them as leaders of the people.

> . . . Let these be at the service of the people to administer justice at all times. They can refer all difficult questions to you, but all smaller questions they will decide for themselves; so making things easier for you, and sharing the burden with you.

The father-in-law is a wise man indeed! He knows that Moses cannot carry the whole people on his shoulders alone. He has to delegate responsibility and share his charism if he is to survive and use his gifts fully for the sake of God's people.

When I speak on prayer and discernment, I always recommend that anyone who is serious about interior growth should have a spiritual director. And the invariable retort — whether in Ireland or the Philippines or the United States — is that good directors are almost as rare as "hen's teeth." If this is true, it may be because those of us who are directors have failed to heed Moses' father-in-law. This, at least, is the conviction which has guided my own ministry and teaching, and which occasions the writing of this book. Moses must do two things: first, give the people the clear principles and "words" of Yahweh which they need as guidelines in the concrete circumstances of their lives; and, second, choose and train able men and women who can share the burden of "judging" the problems of God's people. The father-in-law of Moses ends his advice with a consoling promise which is also meant for us today: "If you do this — and may God so command you — you will be able to stand the strain, and all these people will go home satisfied."

The When and the What

Fortunately, the church has given us a Moses in the person of St. Ignatius Loyola, whose special charism it was to put in writing for the Christian community the basic principles of discerning love. In chapter 3 we explained the context of Ignatius' discussion of discernment in the *Spiritual Exercises*, and we saw that the basic disposition of "simplicity of intention" (which we have called openness to God) is his starting point. He then goes on to discuss (#170-174) the "matters about which a choice should be made," indicating that we do not question "unchangeable" choices (e.g., marriage, priesthood) which have been made validly. Nor do we re-examine changeable decisions if we have already "made a choice properly and with due order." These comments may seem too obvious to need stating, but I have found that the devil can wreak havoc with good people by urging them to question repeatedly and worry about choices already made. Often such people are vulnerable because their image of God is that of the puppeteer, or better the Father of small children, sitting in heaven inflexibly holding to his will and punishing those who, even in good faith, have failed to read his mind correctly. We human beings do behave in that way; but mercifully, as we have seen in chapter 1, our God does not.

Ignatius' advice in such cases is eminently sane and liberating. Where the choice was well and sincerely made — and, as we shall see, this does not necessarily mean it was "correct," objectively the best choice, since we rarely have that kind of certitude about faith decisions (cf. chapter 3) — then, Ignatius says, "there seems to be no reason why we should make it over. But let him perfect himself as much as possible in the one he has made." Even in the case of a decision improperly made but unchangeable (Ignatius mentions as examples marriage or the priesthood), he says, "since it cannot be undone, no further choice is possible." This may seem to contradict our present practice, with dispensations from priestly celibacy and marriage annulments (or even separations) much more commonly obtainable. However, I do not believe there is a contradiction. What can be "undone" may vary at various times in the church's history, since she is rooted in a concrete and changing sociological and psychological milieu. But bad choices are always a tragedy, even though the ways of handling the tragedy may change.[1] Ignatius' point is not to specify which decisions are unchangeable, but to tell us how to

---

1 Surprisingly, Ignatius' thinking is singularly modern, even though he does not discuss, or imply, our contemporary pastoral and juridical practices. He does, that is, seem to lay the foundation for the church's more "lenient" approach today when he says: "Since such an (unchangeable) choice was inordinate and awry, it does not seem to be a vocation from God, as many erroneously believe. They make a divine call out of a perverse and wicked choice. For every vocation that comes from God is always pure and undefiled, uninfluenced by the flesh or any inordinate attachment" (#173). The God of Ignatius, it seems, is not only all-holy but remarkably "mature" in the freedom to err which he gives to his children.

behave whenever a truly unchangeable decision has been made. Of such a case he says: "If the (unchangeable) choice has not been made as it should have been, and with due order, that is, if it was not made without inordinate attachments, one should be sorry for this, and take care to live well in the life he has chosen." The goodness of this God of ours is perhaps most strikingly evident in his willingness to write straight with our crooked lines.

This is not, of course, to canonize sin or to suggest that we should deliberately make unwise and "crooked" choices in order to further elicit God's mercy. We will make plenty of mistakes without trying to. And, as Paul insists in Romans 6, those who truly love, and who truly experience God's forgiving love in Christ Jesus, can only desire to be conformed more and more to this love in their own free choices. For Ignatius, too, this is the central concern. And so his discussion focuses on matters which are still open to choice for the soul rooted in God's love. The whole thrust of the *Spiritual Exercises* up to this point (the end of the second week) is to bring the soul to a total openness to whatever the Lord desires of her. If changeable choices have been improperly made, that is, not "sincerely and with due order, then, if one desires to bring forth fruit that is worthwhile and most pleasing in the sight of God our Lord, it will be profitable to (now) make a choice in the proper way" (#174). And if the choice has not yet been made—if, for example, the soul is still free to choose either marriage or the single lay life or the religious life when she comes to this genuine openness to God's will for her—then such a soul is doubly blessed. She has no bad choices to regret or reform, and the climate is ideal for a good choice.

In such situations, St. Ignatius stresses one important point about the "what" of such choices. He says, "It is necessary that all matters of which we wish to make a choice be either indifferent or good in themselves, and such that they are lawful within our Holy Mother, the hierarchical church, and not bad or opposed to her" (#170). We have already seen that discernment involves a choice among alternative courses of action, and that it presupposes unclarity as to which course is really God's will. Since, however, God can never will evil, the alternatives must both be good or, Ignatius says, at least indifferent. Most moral theologians today would doubt that there are any truly "indifferent" (i.e., neither morally good nor morally bad but somehow neutral) alternatives in the concrete situation of choice. Maybe, for example, eating ice cream would be morally indifferent in the abstract. But we never eat ice cream in the abstract! We always eat it with a friend when we are overweight, knowing it was stolen, upon the prescription of a doctor, to celebrate; in short, we always eat it in concrete circumstances which give it a moral coloring. And one who begins the day with the morning offering, and sincerely means what it says, makes *every* act of the day — even eating ice cream — an act of love of God.

Ignatius would have no problem with this recent thinking. In fact, he would be quite in agreement with it. His point is that our discernment can never be a deliberation concerning matters that are evil, since we seek God's will and he can never will what is evil. Thus one could never discern whether to have an abortion or not, whether to join in backbiting or not, whether or not to fornicate or to lie. To do so would be an insult to our God, since it would imply that he might desire something evil in itself. This is not to say that we always have a clear perception whether something is good or evil. Although they are wrong, many people today apparently sincerely believe that abortion is morally good in certain circumstances. And even when we know abortion or fornication to be morally wrong, we may have great difficulty determining whether a specific act really is abortion or fornication. For example, would a woman subjected to rape be free to submit passively in order to save her life, or would she be obliged to resist to death? Would such submission be fornication for her? Moral theologians have debated about her obligations and rights for centuries. Or, to give a less dramatic example, how do we draw the line between un-Christian backbiting and legitimate criticism? Sometimes my comments about another to a third person may help me or the third person to help our friend or acquaintance, and sometimes such comments may merely destroy or undermine his good name. The difference might be clear on occasion, but at other times it can be very difficult to draw the line.

Thus, determining the moral goodness of certain courses of action can be extremely difficult. But this in no way questions the principle of Ignatius concerning legitimate matters for discernment: We can never discern between alternative choices when one (or both) of the alternatives is morally evil. What we have seen is that it may not always be easy to determine whether the alternatives are indeed morally good and thus legitimate options for discernment. In this case we may have to discern whether we really have matter for discernment! That is, we may have to bring the doubtful alternative to the Lord as we see it, and tell him we are not sure whether this is even a possible choice, but we trust him to make his will clear to us.

It might also be necessary for us to seek further *information* about the doubtful alternative. For example, we might need to ask reputable moralists or informed priests what is the church's teaching on questions like rape or indirect abortion. This gathering of data is not discernment proper; but often it is a necessary preliminary to discernment, especially for persons whom the Lord has given sufficient intelligence to weigh the facts, and who have access to proper sources of information concerning the principles involved. God's will for us cannot contradict his revelation or the fundamental principles of moral law.

To understand better the difference between this "data gathering" and discernment proper, let us now turn to consider St. Ignatius' famous discussion of the three occasions for making a proper choice in accordance with God's will. At times, I believe, a misunderstanding of these occasions has led to confusion concerning the difference between reasoning and discernment.

The How of Discernment

Having discussed the proper dispositions and the legitimate matters for a good discernment, St. Ignatius then presents the retreatant making the *Spiritual Exercises* with "three times or occasions, when a correct and good choice of a way of life may be made." Although a retreat is the ideal situation for these three "times" to occur, especially in making critical decisions such as the choice of a state of life, any of the three can be realized in daily life as well. The first, which we may call a "revelation time," is ideal but fairly rare, while the third is, as we shall see, not properly discernment but is very close to what we have just called data gathering or reasoning. Thus we could call this third time a "reasoning time."

The first or "revelation time" for making a good choice, then, is "when God our Lord so moves and attracts the will that a devout soul without hesitation, or the possibility of hesitation, follows what has been manifested to it" (#175). In this case God's will is so clear that the soul cannot doubt what he wants. St. Ignatius says, by way of example, that "St. Paul and St. Matthew acted thus in following Christ our Lord." His point in citing St. Paul seems clear enough, when we recall Paul's experience on the road to Damascus; he was stricken from his horse, blinded, and addressed directly by one who said, "I am Jesus, and you are persecuting me. Get up now and go into the city, and you will be told what you have to do" (Acts 9:5). The power of God was then so tangible in his life, and the word of Jesus so clear, that Paul could scarcely doubt what the Lord wanted of him.

Ignatius' mention of Matthew is more puzzling, or at least it was to me for many years. But the point seems to be that in all three of the synoptics Matthew's call is very simple and direct, and he follows Jesus without any doubt or hesitation. "As Jesus was walking on from there he saw a man named Matthew sitting by the customs house and he said to him, 'Follow me.' And he got up and followed him" (Mt 9:9). Again Ignatius implies that St. Matthew's experience of God was so clear and immediate that he could not possibly doubt who was speaking to him or what he wanted. In such "revelation" cases there is no ambiguity, no uncertainty about God's will, and thus there is nothing to discern. Unlike John and Andrew, who observed, questioned, "came and saw," and only then made their discerning decision to remain with him from that time onward (Jn 1:35-39), Matthew seems to have recognized immediately who was calling him and what he was called to do.

This revelation time for making a good choice is not discernment in the strict sense since there is no doubt about God's will and thus nothing to discern. It is an ideal situation, in the sense that God's will is perfectly clear. But it is not the usual way we discover his will. While I believe that sincere pray-ers do occasionally experience such moments of clarity and certitude concerning God's desires for them—whether the experience be dramatic like Paul's or matter-of-fact like Matthew's—the more usual situation, even for the saints, involves a much larger dose of the obscurity of faith.

In contrast with the "peak" moments of Ignatius' first time of clear revelation, the third or "reasoning" time for making a good choice is one in which there is great uncertainty concerning God's will. The two are similar in that in both cases there is nothing to discern. But, in the third, this "nothing" is a frustrating nothing; that is, in contrast with the clarity and certainty of the revelation time, here God does not seem to be saying *anything* to the soul sincerely seeking his will. This is the way St. Ignatius describes it: "This (third time) is a time of tranquillity. . . . I said it is a time of tranquillity, that is, a time when the soul is not agitated by different spirits and has free and peaceful use of its natural powers" (#177). The language here is tricky, since "tranquillity" sounds like a good sign. In fact, as we shall see, tranquillity or peace is one of the key marks of the presence of the Spirit of God. Here, however, the word has quite a different connotation.

For many years, I was puzzled and confused by this third, reasoning time, particularly since directors and commentators often seemed to present it as the ideal discerning situation. Ignatius suggests that one experiencing such "tranquillity" use his or her natural powers of reasoning and imagination to weigh the pros and cons of the situation and come to a tentative decision concerning God's will. He even gives two detailed methods for doing this. The problem I saw was that these methods do not seem to correspond to the rules for discernment which Ignatius gives us in the same *Spiritual Exercises*. Those rules speak of feelings, of consolations and desolations, of good and evil spirits working; but here in the reasoning time, we seem to be in a world not of feeling but of calm rational analysis. One method for this reasoning time speaks of recalling first the matter to be decided and then the end for which I am created. In a spirit of indifference or detachment, I should then, after prayer for light and courage, "use the understanding to weigh the matter with care and fidelity, and make my choice in conformity with what would be more pleasing to his most holy will" (#180). Ignatius, practical man that he is, suggests doing this by enumerating the advantages and disadvantages of each alternative (e.g., to enter the religious life, to stay single, or to marry). And then:

> After I have gone over and pondered in this way every aspect of the matter in question, I will consider which alternative appears more reasonable. Then I must come to a decision in the matter under deliberation because of weightier motives presented to my reason, and not because of any sensual inclination (#182).

This is a very logical way to resolve uncertainty about one's course of action, and we could easily use it even in purely secular matters or without God entering the picture. The second way of making a good choice in this reasoning time when we are using our natural powers is less logical but no less natural. It involves the imagination and—as I realize now—contrasts with the first "reasoning" way above as does contemplation with meditation.[2] Ignatius suggests three imaginative exercises: First, to consider what I would advise another person who came to me facing the same choice which I now face; second, to imagine myself on my deathbed and ask what I would then wish to have chosen; or, finally, "let me picture and consider myself as standing in the presence of my judge on the last day (the final judgment) and reflect what decision in the present matter I would then wish to have made" (#187). In each case I get some light on my present confusion by imaginatively distancing myself from it. Sometimes it is quite clear to us, for example, what advice we would give another person facing a dilemma similar to our own. And yet we cannot apply the same to ourselves. Many times people have asked my advice, and, upon hearing it, have said: "How strange! I have said that to others. Why could I not see it as applicable to myself?" The reason, of course, is that we find it difficult to distance ourselves from our own problems and to look at them "objectively."

Both of Ignatius' "reasoning time" ways—the more properly rational weighing of the pros and cons, and the more imaginative projection which we have just explained—are effective means of

---

2 Cf. *Opening to God*, ch. 6. Both Ignatian contemplation and meditation are beginners' ways of "getting to know" God, but meditation uses the understanding whereas contemplation, in the Ignatian sense, uses the imagination.

coming to a decision in this time of "tranquillity," when God seems to be leaving us to our natural powers. And yet I have said they are not properly discernment. They involve listening to our own hearts, to our own better judgment, rather than to God's voice. But, you might ask, isn't our own better judgment the way God speaks to us? Haven't we stressed that God works through and in collaboration with his creatures—that grace builds on nature? Unless we are going to start looking for miraculous voices and visions, would it not seem that these techniques of reasoning and imagination are the normal way one would seek to discover God's will?

Discernment Proper: Ignatius' "Second Time"

There is no doubt that most good people do make faith decisions in the two natural, "reasoning time" ways just described. And they believe that they are discerning. Moreover, they are correct in thinking that we should not normally seek for miraculous visions and voices as a guide to Christian decision making. Such miraculous signs would, if genuine, be such clear interventions of God in our lives that no doubt about his will would be possible. In other words, they would be instances of St. Ignatius' "first time" for making a good choice, a time of clear revelation which is rather rare and in which no discernment is needed.

The problem is that there is a neglected middle way between the clarity of the revelation time and the free and calm use of our natural powers in the reasoning time. There is a "second time" and Ignatius describes it thus: "Second time. When much light and understanding are derived through the experience of desolations and consolations and the discernment of diverse spirits" (#176). This is the only one of the three times or occasions for making a good choice which Ignatius calls "discernment." Moreover, at the end of both of the procedures, the logical and the imaginative, which he gives us above for the use of our natural powers of reasoning and imagination in tranquillity, he adds this instruction: "After such a choice or decision, the one who has made it must turn with great diligence to prayer in the presence of God our Lord, and offer him his choice that the

Divine Majesty may deign to accept and confirm it if it is for his greater service and praise."[3] That is, the soul who has come to a tentative choice by means of the natural rational or imaginative methods which Ignatius describes, must then present the choice to the Lord for his confirmation. And how would he confirm it? By the "consolations and desolations" of the second time, by discernment proper; unless, that is, we are blessed with the unusual "revelation time" experience of a Paul or a Matthew.

This implies that what most devout people do when faced with an important decision — namely, try to "figure out" what God wants of them — is not wrong, but it is incomplete. Sometimes we will be directly moved as if by an inspiration from the Lord, to a certain decision or course of action. More often, though, we will need to use our own heads first to determine what is best, and *then* submit our tentative conclusion to the Lord for his confirmation. Or else we will have to discriminate between, discern conflicting inspirations to act. But whichever way it happens, the "inspiration" or "confirmation" is something quite different from our own reasoning and imagining. It is, to put it quite simply, the difference between guessing what my friend is thinking and hearing him *say* what he is thinking!

But how does God say what he is thinking? We do not hear him as we hear our human friends. Nor can we look into his eyes as we look into theirs. This, as we have already seen in chapter 3, is the crucial problem of discernment. At this point in the *Spiritual Exercises*, St. Ignatius merely gives us a tantalizing clue to its solution, when he says that "much light and understanding are derived through the experience of desolations and consolations." Whatever these desolations and consolations are, they are the raw material of discernment. Ignatius tells us no more about them in discussing the "three times for a good choice"; fortunately, however, he returns to the topic in his famous Rules for Discernment of Spirits at the end of the *Spiritual Exercises*. Let us now turn to those rules, and thus to discernment proper.

---

3 #183. This concludes the more meditative (logical) method of weighing the pros and cons. At the end of the more contemplative, imaginative method (#188), Ignatius simply refers us back to #183.

Practicum Question

Let us recall Sister Letty (chapter 3) and her problem concerning evangelization and justice in her religious congregation. In the light of what we have seen in chapter 4, how would you *begin* the process of co-discernment with her? Would you advise her to leave the congregation? Or to stop questioning and simply obey superiors? If neither, would it be good to begin by suggesting one of the two methods (weighing the pros and cons, or imagining herself, for example, advising a friend in the congregation) of Ignatius' "third time"?

Chapter 5
The Tactics of God and the Enemy

We have said that only the second of St. Ignatius' three times for making a good choice is properly discernment. The first time is so clear that no discernment is needed; in the third there are no "consolations and desolations," no "diverse spirits" to discern. In the latter case we are left to our natural powers of reasoning and imagination. We pray for light and the guidance of the Holy Spirit, but it seems we are left to our own resources in coming to a decision. We hope and trust that the Spirit is behind the scenes, as it were, guiding our decision-making process even though his presence is not felt. And St. Ignatius tells us that this indirect, hoped-for guidance of God should not suffice. Even though it may be necessary for us to use our own resources, especially when God does seem silent and unconcerned about our questions to him, Ignatius does not want us to stop there. Having come to a tentative decision in this "natural" way, we must then bring our decision to the Lord and ask him to "accept and confirm it if it is for his greater service and praise" (#183). This can only mean, as we have seen in chapter 4, returning to the "second time," to discernment proper.

Thus we may discern directly at times, and at other times we may have to do some spadework first — gathering data, reflecting, weighing alternatives — before actually discerning. In either case, discernment proper, as the "second time" (#176) tells us, consists of the "experience of desolations and consolations and discernment of diverse spirits." To understand, then, what discernment is it would seem we need a clear grasp of the meaning of "desolations and consolations" and of what these "diverse spirits" are. Fortunately St. Ignatius tells us, in his characteristically spare and methodical manner, in his famous Rules for the Discernment of Spirits (#313-336). These are by far the most important of a series of practical guidelines for living which he appends to the *Spiritual Exercises,* the others being: Rules for the Distribution of Alms (#337-344); Some Notes Concerning Scruples (#345-351); and Rules for Thinking With the Church (#352-370).

Before we turn to the rules for discernment proper, it might be helpful to know how St. Ignatius came to formulate these now-classic guidelines for Christian life and decision making. He was not a speculative thinker but an eminently practical man of action. This is not to say, however, that he did not think; like any of the great constructive "doers" of history, he thought much, not about abstract schemata or ultimate explanations but about the meaning of his own and others' concrete experience. He was concerned with the patterns of this experience, especially our experience of God working in our lives, with a view to responding better, cooperating better with him. It has been said that the great thinkers of the continental European speculative traditions "live to think," whereas the great figures of the Anglo-Saxon tradition "think to live." For the latter, thought is pragmatic, at the service of the good life. If this be so, then St. Ignatius Loyola would be solidly in the Anglo-Saxon tradition!

Because of this strong pragmatic, experiential bent, his writing is firmly grounded in his own life experience, and nowhere more so than in his guidelines for discernment. In 1555, toward the end of his life, St. Ignatius narrated to Father Gonzalez de Camara, one of the early Jesuits, his own early experiences with discernment. His conversion to a holy life began on his sickbed after the battle of Pamplona in 1521. Having seen his dreams of military glory shattered along with his leg, he was suffering through a long and frustrating convalescence when his sister-in-law provided him with some pious books to read. One of them was a life of some of the great medieval saints, among whom Dominic, Francis and Onofrio (Humphrey) stirred his imagination. He began to daydream of doing the great deeds they had done—no longer for an earthly king but for the King of Heaven. Not all was grandeur and glory though; there were times when he was high and times when he was depressed and discouraged—a normal enough experience for any human being.

In Ignatius' case, however, these alternating periods of "consolation and desolation" were to have momentous consequences for the church.

Father Joseph Pegon, S.J., summarizes Ignatius' reminiscences to Gonzalez de Camara:[1]

> In 1555 Ignatius told Gonzalez de Camara how his conversion had begun by alternating periods of exaltation and depression; it was a new experience for a soldier-sinner, the result of holy reading. Ignatius did not stop to scrutinize these variations of personal feeling until one day his eyes were opened. . . . His experience led him to the conclusion that certain thoughts made him sad, others joyous. Little by little he realized the difference between the spirits that moved him, the spirit of the devil and the Spirit of God . . . such were the first reflections that he, Ignatius, made on the things of God.

This discovery about his own experience and the diverse "spirits" at work in his feelings was to become the core of the *Spiritual Exercises*. They are, above all, an exercise in "discerning love." And Ignatius firmly believed that it was God himself who taught him, like a schoolboy, how to apply the norms of discerning love, of discernment, first to his own religious experience and then to that of others. Father Jules Toner, S.J., in an excellent new commentary on the rules for discernment, quotes from Ignatius' Autobiography (#27), as narrated in the third person to Gonzalez de Camara:

> At this time God treated him just as a schoolmaster treats a little boy when he teaches him. This was perhaps because of his rough and uncultivated understanding, or because he had no one to teach him, or because of the firm will God had given him in his service. But he clearly saw, and always had seen that God dealt with him like this. Rather, he thought that any doubt about it would be

---

1 *Discernment of Spirits*, Guillet *et al.*, p. 80. Pegon wrote chapter 4, "The Modern Period," of this classic article on discernment in the *Dictionnaire de Spiritualite*. In chapters 1 and 2 we made extensive use of Father Jacques Guillet's chapter on "Sacred Scripture." The original source here is the *Fontes Narrativi de S. Ignacio de Loyola*, to which Pegon makes reference. See also *The Spirituality of St. Ignatius Loyola* by Hugo Rahner, S.J. (Trans., Francis J. Smith, S.J.), Loyola U. Press, 1953, pp. 22-35.

an offense against his Divine Majesty.[2]

Apparently Ignatius had the kind of certainty about God's teaching which he attributes to St. Paul and St. Matthew in the "first time" for making a good choice.

This gift of God to Ignatius was, however, purchased at a high price. As Pegon says of the saint's experience after his conversion: "Later, at Manresa, these interior alternating movements became more intense, led to an attack of scruples and a temptation to suicide; these variations gave him the occasion to note 'how this spirit had entered into him.' " There were still times of light alternating with the darkness, until finally

> . . . a famous vision on the shore of the (River) Cardoner provided the decisive light: he "began to see everything with different eyes and *to distinguish and experience good and evil spirits.*" At the same time, the saint "began to share with others the meditations and spiritual exercises in which he had special grace and efficacy and the gift of discernment of spirits."[3]

Ignatius' conversion story has been told and retold in succeeding centuries, and is probably almost as well known now as those of St. Francis of Assisi and St. Paul himself. Our purpose in recalling it here is to underline the experiential character of the rules for discernment. They were Ignatius' attempt to put into writing, for the guidance of others, what he himself had learned at Loyola and Manresa and by the Cardoner, and eventually in Salamanca and Paris as God continued to teach his itinerant "schoolboy." The rules, so few (14 for the first week and eight for the second) and so lapidary, were written in his own sweat and blood. Let us now see if we can "unpack" them and recapture the experiential richness which went into their writing.

---

2 Jules J. Toner, S.J., *A Commentary on St. Ignatius' Rules for the Discernment of Spirits: A Guide to the Principles and Practice*, p. 8 (St. Louis, Mo.: Institute of Jesuit Sources, 1982). Toner's work is more technical and scholarly than our present work. It would be difficult to read through from cover to cover, but is an excellent reference source, particularly for directors who wish to have at their fingertips the fruits of the best research, classic and contemporary, on specific topics treated in the rules. Cf. Toner's own explanation of his "intent" on p. 17.

3 Pegon, *op. cit.*, p. 80. The vision by the Cardoner is one of the most famous in the history of spirituality and is attested to by several of Ignatius' early companions, including James Laynez whom Pegon is quoting here.

What's in a Title?

Ignatius provides two sets of rules for discernment, one "more suited to the first week" of the *Spiritual Exercises*, when the soul faces the challenge to be radically open and "naked" before the Lord, and the other set "more suitable for the second week," when the focus shifts from self-knowledge to the knowledge of God in Christ Jesus. He gives the following lengthy title to the first-week rules: "Rules for understanding to some extent the different movements produced in the soul and for recognizing those that are good to admit them, and those that are bad, to reject them. These rules are more suited to the first week" (#313).

As we have said, the first week of the *Spiritual Exercises* corresponds to the situation of beginners in the spiritual life. Generally speaking, the retreatant of the first week will be a good person in the sense that he or she takes God seriously enough to desire a 30-day retreat. But, while desirous of growing, such a person is not very deep. Like Francis Xavier at the time of his conversion retreat, he or she has never really gone below the surface of life and come face to face with who God really is and who I really am. The first week is a time of opening to God in a whole new way. It is a move from the servant level to the friend level, and the first fruit of this move is, paradoxically, a painful awareness of how small a role God has really played in my life until now. Jesus' confrontation with the pious Nicodemus (Jn 3) can serve as a good analogy for the experience of the retreatant of the first week: Nicodemus comes in sincere search of the truth, but he finds his whole world turned upside down. Jesus' gaze strips him naked and reveals how smug he has been, how falsely complacent concerning his own righteousness.

The first week, then, is a painful, costly time, even though the pain is bittersweet for one really seeking the truth. For this reason, we will not be surprised to learn that these rules — "more suited to the first week" — deal almost entirely with desolation. The devil's way with beginners, who experience the shaking of the comfortable foundations of their lives, will be to try to discourage them. He will present every possible argument to convince the beginner that the demands of self-knowledge are unreasonable, psychologically unhealthy, too heavy for the ordinary person to bear. As we shall see, the devil has to change his tactics with committed souls of the second week, where the rules will focus instead on true and false consolation. For the present, though, we merely note that what Ignatius sees as more suited to the beginner is clear guidance concerning desolation.

Before turning to these guidelines, let us also note the phrase with which the first week rules begin: "Rules for understanding to some extent the different movements. . . ." The words "to some extent" are important, though I had lived with the *Spiritual Exercises* and these rules for discernment for many years without even noticing them. Why "to some extent"? Because discernment is always gradual and reformable. God reveals his will to us step by step. He does not give us a total, long-range blueprint of his will for us. Nor does he normally give us infallible advance certainty regarding his will. Rather, as we noted in chapter 3 when speaking of the courage required of a good discerner, the ultimate test of our discernment is our experience. Even in the second week, where the soul is more mature and deeper in the knowledge of God and his ways, the rules give us a "more accurate discernment" (#328) — still not infallible, if I read Ignatius correctly, but more accurate than was possible to a beginner. This also corresponds to my own experience as a pray-er and as a director. The Lord, it seems, wants us to move ahead in faith, to take the next step indicated without seeing clearly where it will ultimately lead us. Oftentimes a young man seeking to discern his vocation will want to know the final outcome: If I apply to join the Franciscans, will I be accepted? If accepted, will I persevere? And will I be a good religious and priest? It is what we call in the Philippines the "Sigurista" mentality — the desire to be sure of the landing before I leap — and is a quite normal human reaction in the face of risk. Our God, however, does not seem to want to work this way. He reveals his will step by step and asks us to entrust the future to him. I discern whether to apply to the Franciscans. If I am not accepted, that does not mean my well-made discernment to apply was a mistake. The only mistake, perhaps, is my projection beyond the next step, my inference as to the long-range will of God. He never told me I would die a Franciscan; all he told me was to apply! If I made the best judgment I could in a prayerful and discerning spirit, the Lord is pleased with my response to his call. Living by faith, I only read his will "to some extent." The rest is up to him.

Desolation and Consolation

We have seen the implications of two important phrases in the title of the rules of the first week: "to some extent" and "more suited to the first week." The final phrase needing explanation, and the one that brings us to the very heart of discernment proper, is "the different movements produced in the soul." It is these "movements" which we discern; our attentiveness to them is what differentiates discernment from ordinary decision making, or even from the natural methods recommended by Ignatius for the "time of tranquillity" when there are no movements of soul to discern.

But what are these "different movements produced in the soul"? Ignatius tells us in the third and fourth rules of this first week (#316-317). He calls them "spiritual consolation" and "spiritual desolation." In the third rule he defines consolation as follows:

> I call it consolation when an interior movement is aroused in the soul, by which it is inflamed with love of its Creator and Lord, and as a consequence, can love no creature on the face of the earth for its own sake, but only in the Creator of them all. It is likewise consolation when one sheds tears that move to the love of God, whether it be because of sorrow for sins, or because of the sufferings of Christ our Lord, or for any other reason that is immediately directed to the praise and service of God. Finally, I call consolation every increase of faith, hope and love, and all interior joy that invites and attracts to what is heavenly and to the salvation of one's soul by filling it with peace and quiet in its Creator and Lord.

Thus consolation can take many forms: It may involve strong emotion — being inflamed with love, shedding tears of love and praise — or it may be quiet and deep. The common denominator, I would say, is *peace* in the Lord; whether the soul be deeply and strongly moved, as in the emotional reunion of two lovers after a long separation, or quietly consoled, as might be the experience of a mother gazing on the sleeping form of her newborn child in the middle of the night and quietly marveling at the wonder of life which has come from her body — in either case, the strongly emotional or the quietly deep, the defining quality which makes it consolation is peace. In the case of spiritual consolation, this will be a peace in the Lord, a felt increase of faith, hope and love, of interior joy drawing me to him.[4]

Note that all of the words which St. Ignatius uses to describe consolation are *feeling* words. It is the feelings we discern and not the thoughts. There is perhaps no point about discernment which is so little realized or understood as this, especially in cultures and religious traditions where feelings are given little value or are considered suspect. It is the feelings, the felt awareness of God, which are lacking in the "tranquillity" of Ignatius' third time for making a good choice. Then, because there are no feelings to discern, we must fall back on our reasoning and try to come to a decision by weighing the pros and cons, or by an imaginative projection of the consequences of our possible choices. But this is not discernment, as we have seen in chapter 4, and when we have come to a tentative decision by these means, we must then bring it to the Lord and ask him to confirm it. How would he confirm it? By the felt experience of consolation with which he moves the soul.

The natural and logical objection at this point is this: But can we trust our feelings? Aren't they notoriously tricky and deceptive? Is that not the reason why so many of us have been taught to "transcend" our feelings and to make choices rationally and with cool heads? This is true; our feelings are treacherous, but they are also crucial. To suppress or seek to transcend or ignore them is to throw out the baby with the bath water. The cure is worse than the illness, as many of us raised in a rigid, duty-bound religious tradition have learned to our grief.

What, then, is the solution? In the first place we must recognize that the feelings are essential to our spiritual life and to

---

4 On peace as the "core" of every *spiritual* consolation, cf., Toner, *op. cit.*, pp. 87 ff.

our discovery of God's will for us. But, secondly, we must also realize that the feelings *are* treacherous and cannot be blindly trusted or followed. The past 15 or 20 years have seen a swing of the pendulum from joyless pursuit of duty to "letting it all hang out." By now reflective people should see clearly that the cult of feelings, in spirituality as in secular life, which has characterized recent years is at least as destructive as the earlier repression of feeling. The proper balance, as St. Ignatius saw 400 years ago, is *discernment* of our religious feelings. The feelings are crucial: They are the raw material of our experience of God. But they must be judged, rationally evaluated to distinguish the weeds from the wheat.

The complexity of our feelings can perhaps be seen best by noting that Ignatius refers not only to consolation but also to desolation. In rule 4 he defines desolation thus:

> I call desolation what is entirely the opposite of what is described in the third rule, as darkness of soul, turmoil of spirit, inclination to what is low and earthly, restlessness arising from many disturbances which lead to lack of faith, lack of hope, lack of love. The soul is wholly slothful, tepid, sad, and separated, as it were, from its Creator and Lord. For just as consolation is the opposite of desolation, so the thoughts that spring from consolation are the opposite of those that spring from desolation.

Thus desolation is the very opposite of consolation. And like consolation it can take various forms, from emotional turmoil of spirit to a deadening tepidity and sadness. The common note of all forms of desolation, I believe, is the *loss of peace*. Whether the feelings be stormy or simply "blah," the absence of peace will mark desolation just as surely as the experience of peace marks consolation.

Both consolation and desolation, then, are feeling states, and lead to thoughts or inspirations to act; as we stressed earlier, discernment is where prayer meets action. Our experience of God, if it is genuine, always leads to action, to a return of love. The "action" may be to pray longer or to volunteer for the missions; it may be very ordinary or it may mark a turning point in our life. But, as the Epistle of James (2:14-26) makes clear, faith (or love or hope) without good works is dead. St. Teresa of Avila, speaking as a cloistered contemplative, insisted that the important thing in prayer is "not to think much but to love much,"[5] and that love does not consist in beautiful feelings but in a great and efficacious desire to do the will of God. We can thus say that discernment involves the whole person: feelings, intellect and will. The feelings are the raw material which we discern; it is the intellect which judges the source and validity of these feelings; and it is the will which is moved to act on the basis of this judgment. Without the feelings, the whole process of discernment has no content.

Our Fundamental Option

The faithful pray-er, then, must be in touch with his or her feelings. Moreover, he or she must have some grounds for judging whence these feelings come and whether they are a sound basis for Spirit-inspired action. The rules for discernment are, very simply, the norms St. Ignatius (like St. Paul and St. John before him) gives us for so judging. Most of these rules are detailed and specific, but before entering into the details Ignatius discusses two distinct and contrasting states of soul—two basic orientations, which today we would call "fundamental options." The first is that of a soul who goes "from one mortal sin to another" (#314), that is, whose fundamental option in life is against God and for self. With such persons, "the enemy is ordinarily accustomed to propose apparent pleasures. He fills their imagination with sensual delights and gratifications (i.e., with apparent consolations), the more readily to keep them in their vices and increase the number of their sins." The good spirit, God, whose action is always opposed to that of the "enemy," will do the opposite: "Making use of the light of reason, he will rouse the sting of conscience and fill them with remorse (i.e., with apparent desolation)." Thus one whose fundamental option is against God will be "consoled" by the devil and disturbed by God. Why? Because the devil wishes to maintain the present course and direction of the soul, whereas the good Lord wishes to shake her out of her evil complacency.

Just the reverse is true for souls "who go on earnestly striving

---

5 The *Interior Castle*, Fourth Mansions, ch 1.

to cleanse their souls from sin and who seek to rise in the service of God our Lord to greater perfection" (#315). Such souls have chosen God and his service as the basic orientation of their lives. They may fail in many ways—the just man sins seven times a day—but their fundamental option is for God. In such a case, disturbance or desolation comes from the devil and peace from God:

> Then it is characteristic of the evil spirit to harass with anxiety, to afflict with sadness, to raise obstacles backed by fallacious reasonings that disturb the soul. Thus he seeks to prevent the soul from advancing. On the other hand, it is characteristic of the good spirit to give courage and strength, consolations, tears, inspirations, and peace. This he does by making all easy, by removing all obstacles so that the soul goes forward in doing good.

This insight of Ignatius concerning the diverse ways the good and evil spirits work, depending on the fundamental life commitment of the soul, is of extreme importance in practice. It explains why persons apparently committed to an evil life seem to be serene in their wrongdoing. If they are stubborn enough in their refusal of grace, the good spirit may well give up on them; they can, as it were, "kill their conscience." The evil spirit will do everything possible to avoid rocking the boat. He will lull them into a false sense of security; he will convince them of the value of the perquisites of power and of the pleasures of the flesh. He will even, as C. S. Lewis notes in his masterpiece on discernment, *The Screwtape Letters*, persuade them that he, the devil, does not exist! In short, he will use every means to preserve the complacency, the pseudoconsolation, of the soul going "from mortal sin to mortal sin."

By contrast, the soul truly committed to God will find the devil working overtime to shake his or her commitment. And the Lord will do everything possible to encourage the soul to persevere in the basic orientation of life it has chosen. Thus, for example, a person who is sincerely seeking to serve the Lord in a religious community may have many failings and shortcomings. The Lord will seek to correct these and to purify the person's commitment. But he will never act in such a way as to call into question his or her fundamental commitment to God. The devil, though, will do precisely this. He will seek to discourage the person, to convince her that she is a failure, that God is displeased, that the whole enterprise is a mistake.

In Rule 7 of week two (#335), St. Ignatius returns to this question of fundamental option. There he compares the action of the various "spirits" to water falling on a sponge and on a stone. "When the disposition (of the soul) is contrary to that of the spirits, they enter with noise and commotion that are easily perceived," like water falling on a rock. But "when the disposition is similar to that of the spirits, they enter silently, as one coming into his own house when the doors are open," or like water penetrating a sponge. Thus we see that the essential distinction between the two types of souls—those going from mortal sin to mortal sin and those sincerely seeking to love and serve God—determines how the various spirits will work in their lives. It remains to be clarified how this distinction can be applied to concrete experiences of consolation and desolation.

Note, however, that St. Ignatius, having distinguished the two types of fundamental option, gives rules applicable only to the second, to the situation of a soul committed to love and serve the Lord. He never gives guidelines—apart from the general principles which we have just considered—for the soul going from mortal sin to mortal sin. The reason for this omission is evident, I believe: Such a soul would not make a 30-day retreat, nor would she sincerely seek guidance in discerning God's will for her. If, by some chance, she did enter a serious retreat or seek direction, she would not long persevere in the process of self-confrontation which such direction necessarily entails. The committed soul may have many failings. Some of these failings may even be frustratingly deep rooted and persistent,[6] but her commitment, her fundamental option, is genuine and sincere. As long as that is true—whatever her failures in living out concretely this sincere choice for God—the action of the good spirit will always be gentle, sweet and light, and that of the evil spirit disturbing and noisy.

---

6 We have discussed this matter in chapter 2 of *When the Well Runs Dry.*

The Good Spirit and the Evil Spirit

The concrete signs of the working of God and the devil will be our topic beginning in chapter 6. Before we turn to them, however, one further point of terminology should be clarified. St. Ignatius speaks of the discernment of "spirits," and he refers to these spirits as "the good spirit" and "the evil spirit." Who or what, precisely, are these two spirits?

With regard to the good spirit, there is not much problem. It is true that, at one point (#329-331), Ignatius does distinguish between God himself and the good angel. As we shall see in chapter 7, he says that only God himself can cause consolation "without any previous cause," whereas consolation with a preceding cause can come from either the "good angel" or the evil spirit. The distinction between God's work and the good angel's action seems to have been common in medieval theology, since St. John of the Cross also makes the same point. When the experience is sensible, in the senses, it is accomplished by God through the work of his angels; when, however, the soul is directly touched without the mediation of the senses, it can only be God himself working directly and without any angel intermediary. The distinction is not very common today, nor does it seem to be of much practical importance. For the theologian it might be important to distinguish the various ways God can interact with body and spirit. But for the pray-er and the director it seems quite sufficient to equate the "good spirit" with God, without concerning ourselves with the possible role the angels might play as the ministers of his gifts. At least in my own ministry the essential question has been whether God is the one working on the soul. I have never found it important to determine whether he was working through angel intermediaries or not.

We can, then, take the "good spirit" as meaning God himself, the Holy Spirit. The identity of the "evil spirit," however, has been much more problematic in recent times. Ignatius identifies him with "the evil one" (#329) or, more frequently, "the enemy" or "our enemy" (#314, 320, 325-27, 329). In #333 he refers to "the evil spirit, the enemy of our progress and eternal salvation"; and in #334 to "the enemy of our human nature." There is little doubt that Ignatius means the devil, whose existence and malevolent activity was as taken for granted in Ignatius' days as in the time of Jesus himself. Today, however, many reflective people question the existence of the devil, or at least they doubt that many of the disturbances traditionally attributed to him are really his work. In these days of depth psychology and psychosomatic medicine, it would appear that the devil received credit for much which is more correctly attributed to our own subconscious and the subtle interplay of mind and body in each of us.

While my own life and ministry have convinced me of the reality of the literal devil (I can't imagine that man could have managed to make such a mess of his world purely by his own natural powers!), still the point about our own subtle ways of deceiving and disturbing ourselves seems valid. Would this, though, invalidate Ignatius' discussion of the work of the evil spirit? I don't think so. It seems to me that, again for the practical purposes of the pray-er and the director, it is not of great importance whether the desolation we experience comes from our own subconscious, from the environment and culture which is the very air we breathe, or from the literal devil. From the point of view of discernment we can take the "evil spirit" or the "devil" to mean whatever forces are working against God, whether they be "natural" or strictly diabolical. It is of legitimate concern to the theologian which impulses are traceable to natural causes and which might be properly supernatural. But when the pray-er recognizes the tail of the snake, he is wise to run away without looking for the rest of it, and to leave the species determination to snake specialists.

Practicum Question:

In this chapter we have stressed the importance of one's "fundamental option," and of being in touch with one's feelings, for genuine discernment. Do you believe, as you reflect upon your own life, that it is possible to be certain about your own fundamental option? How easy do you find it to recognize and "name" your own feelings? Recall a significant experience in your life where it was difficult to know what you really felt.

Chapter 6
Beginners and Desolation

One of the most surprising features of the rules for discernment is that desolation, while it is never a sign of God's voice for those seeking to love and serve him, is nevertheless not a bad sign. That is, it is not necessarily a sign that the Lord is displeased with us or that we are somehow negligent in our commitment to him. In fact, as we hope to show in this chapter, desolation is often a most effective means to purify and deepen our love for God. This is a paradox: Desolation is never *from* God, and yet it can be a most effective means of growth. How can both statements be true? That is really the essential problem of the book of Job, and it is equally central in the life of every committed pray-er and apostle. The dark night, or dry well or cloud of unknowing, which all refer to the same purifying process experienced by those who are faithful to a life of prayer,[1] is really an experience of desolation, at least in its early stages. While St. John of the Cross is the master teacher and authority on this more advanced form of desolation, St. Ignatius treats of it primarily as it is experienced in the lives of beginners. For both of them, desolation plays a crucial role in spiritual growth.

Recall that Ignatius gives us two sets of rules for discernment, one for the "first week" of the *Spiritual Exercises* and the other for the "second week." As we have said, the first week is the time of beginnings — of conversion from a worldly or mediocre life, of honest self-confrontation before God. The second week is a time of commitment, of putting on Christ, of filling our emptiness with the fullness of Jesus. His values and attitudes become ours by the grace of the second week. Given this contrast between beginnings and more mature commitment, it is striking that Ig-

---

1 As we explained in *When the Well Runs Dry* and *Darkness in the Marketplace*.

natius' rules for the first week — for the time of beginnings — treat almost entirely of desolation, while the rules for the second week treat predominantly of consolation. Apparently St. Ignatius felt that desolation is the normal, or crucial, experience of beginners, and consolation that of more committed souls.

I believe this is true, as an example from my own experience might help to make clear. When I first entered the Jesuit novitiate, at the age of 17, I was homesick for the first four months. The place was strange, I had never known any Jesuits, and only one out of 59 of my class of novices was a fellow Rochesterian. The silence, the rigid routine, the far greater demands in studies than I had known before, the one and one-half hours given daily to personal prayer — everything conspired to make the life seem impossibly hard. It was a fertile field for desolation and the devil made the most of his opportunity. Restlessness, sadness, discouragement and virtually all of the desolation symptoms described by Ignatius were my frequent companions. As I look back, it seems that I alternated between struggling to stay and deciding to leave. And I wasn't really happy with either choice. But then, sometime around Christmas of that first year of novitiate, I awoke one day and realized that I really wanted to stay. There were, of course, many more difficulties and many further adjustments demanded. But they affected me very differently now that I felt I really desired the goal. They were obstacles to be overcome, challenges to be met, rather than reasons to quit.

As the years passed, I became more and more rooted in the life I had chosen. The prayer and religious service of a Jesuit became the central values of my life. At this point, desolation was no longer a great problem or a major part of my prayer experience. Of course there were bad moments and bad days. But even these did not cut very deep, because I learned that bad days did not last very long and the sun always rose again. I discovered that there is genuine wisdom in the old Irishman's solution to every problem: Go to bed! Ninety percent of our problems look much more manageable after a good night's sleep. With this new outlook on my life, I was much less vulnerable to desolation. Unfortunately, though, the devil is shrewd. When we grow, he changes his tactics too. And as we shall see in part III, he works on committed souls not so much by desolation as by false consolation.

Let us not get ahead of ourselves, though. The important point here is that the normal way in which the evil spirit tests and tempts beginners is by desolation — discouragement, anxiety, restlessness, fear, tepidity, in short, by loss of peace. Perhaps we should also note that these "beginnings" may not be only at the very early stage of our life of prayer and commitment. There will be other turning points, for example, when I went to the missions, when a person faces a major change of life (e.g., marriage), when death comes, which are new beginnings for us. In my experience, these are also times when desolation is a significant factor in our discernment.[2]

Rules for Desolation

What we have been saying implies that desolation is the work of the evil spirit, that it is never a sign of God's voice. And this is true, although most people are surprised to hear it. When discouragement and frustration strike, most good people immediately infer that *God* is sending them a message, that perhaps they should give up their work or abandon their vocation. When prayer becomes difficult and dry, it is normal to feel that the Lord has abandoned us and that perseverance is useless. When newlyweds encounter their first difficulties and have their first fight, they easily conclude that they may have made a mistake in marrying. "For better or worse" sounds beautiful in the marriage ceremony, but when the worse comes we realize that it really played no part in our dreams and expectations. Desolation is naturally taken by religious people as a sign that God is displeased with them or disapproves of the course they have chosen.

For this reason, St. Ignatius' first rule for dealing with desolation is both surprising and crucial. He tells us: "In time of desolation we should never make any change but remain firm and constant in the resolution which guided us the day before the

---

2 The "dark nights" of which St. John of the Cross speaks appear to be such a new beginning in the interior life. At these times our prayer life changes radically. We are in a strange new world and the devil again works by desolation.

desolation, or in the decision to which we adhered in the preceding consolation" (#318). If my decision to enter the Jesuits was made prayerfully and in peace, I should never change it while in turmoil or depressed or discouraged. The same applies to seminarian Joe when he is upset about his family situation and begins to question his life in the seminary; or Letty, when she begins to experience the tensions of life in a polarized community; or Ed and Maria when a marriage prayerfully entered into runs into stormy weather. This is not to say that a decision previously made should never be changed, but it should never be changed *in desolation*. Nor should a new decision be made at such a time.

The reason for this, St. Ignatius says, is because "just as in consolation the good spirit guides and counsels us, so in desolation the evil spirit guides and counsels. Following his counsels we can never find the way to a right decision." Desolation is a sign of the evil spirit working; thus we should *never* make or change a decision in desolation unless we want the devil as our spiritual director.[3] So important is this rule that I often tell people to remember it even if they forget everything else they ever hear about discernment. If they remember, and abide by, this one crucial rule in their spirituality, they can eliminate 90 percent of the unhappiness in their lives. Good people make bad decisions because they misinterpret desolation, because they take discouragement, dryness, restlessness as signs of God's will for them. The devil plays on their piety, and their subtle self-pity, by convincing them that their troubles signify God's displeasure with them, or his abandonment of them. Unfortunately the evil spirit is generally much smarter than we are!

What then *should* we do in times of desolation? Granted that we should not make a decision or change our present course, how do we cope? In the next three rules of the first week (#319-321), St. Ignatius makes several suggestions which, in essence, boil down to two main points: working against the desolation by do-

---

3 For simplicity's sake, I refer throughout to the evil spirit as the devil, as "he." Recall, however, that we said in chapter 5 that the "evil spirit" means all those forces working against God and against our growth in his love. Thus the "devil" at work in desolation may be our own unredeemed (and perhaps subconscious) self, or the "world" whose values we drink in with our mother's milk, or the literal devil himself. We will discuss all these "weeds" more fully in chapter 8.

ing the opposite of what the evil spirit suggests; and renewing our faith and trust in the Lord who seems to have abandoned us.

In #319, St. Ignatius says: "Though in desolation we must never change our former resolutions, it will be very advantageous to intensify our activity against the desolation. We can insist more on prayer, upon meditation, and on much examination of ourselves. We can make an effort in a suitable way to do some penance." Ordinarily the evil spirit will seek to turn us away from all these basic Ignatian means to self-knowledge and self-mastery. He will fill us with self-pity and restlessness. At such a time, souls who have a regular prayer life will find their daily 30 minutes for prayer and meditation impossibly long and burdensome. The time given to the examination of conscience will seem utterly wasted. Sometimes the desolation will take the form of discouragement: a sense that God has abandoned the soul and that all efforts to reach or to please him are useless. At other times — perhaps more often today with our activist approach to religious commitment — desolation may appear as a sort of "holy restlessness," a sense that all these pious practices are too self-centered and narcissistic in a world crying for our help. This impatient sense, that the faithful pray-er is like Nero fiddling while Rome burns, is also a form of desolation. Whether the desolation is experienced as quiet desperation or restless impatience, the cause and the appropriate response are the same. The evil spirit, master psychologist that he is, will work on each soul according to its own character: The devout he will discourage and the activist he will make restless. In both cases, the desolation can only come from him.

Since the evil spirit is the source of both types of desolation, we should never follow his inspiration. In fact, as Ignatius is telling us in this #319, the wisest procedure is to do the opposite of what he suggests. This is not to say that we should never shorten our prayer or moderate our penances. There can and will be times when the Lord desires us to do so and the apostolate demands it, but we should never do so in desolation, when our feelings correspond to those Ignatius calls "desolation." At these times we should do the opposite of our inspiration, since the inspiration is from the evil spirit.

An example might help: I often tell committed pray-ers who have reached a certain maturity in their interior lives that the only time they really need to "watch the clock" in their prayer is when they are in desolation. In the beginning we do need the discipline of set times and regular places, as the fox wisely told the Little Prince, since this is the way our hearts are tamed. But once we are tamed and God is important to us, we can generally follow our "inner clock." In times of desolation, however, when the time of prayer seems long and frustrating, it is good to be strict with ourselves. If you normally pray 30 minutes a day, when the half hour seems long and burdensome stay for 31 minutes! Shake your hourglass (like St. Teresa of Avila) to make the time pass faster, if you wish, but stay the full time and a bit longer. Do the opposite of what the devil inspires. After all, what would you do if you were the devil? If your tactics succeeded in reducing 30 minutes to 25 today, you would return to the attack tomorrow and aim for 20 . . . and then 15 . . . 12 . . . 10. . . . But if you, as the devil, only succeeded in making your intended victim pray longer than usual, you would quickly abandon this line of attack. No one has ever accused the devil of being stupid!

St. Ignatius returns to this idea of working against the inspirations of the evil spirit in the eighth rule of this first week (#321). He says, "When one is in desolation, he should strive to persevere in patience. This reacts against the vexations that have overcome him." He also suggests certain useful topics for reflection when one is in desolation. In this rule: "Let him consider, too, that consolation will soon return"; and in the preceding (#320): "he should be mindful that God has left him to his natural powers to resist the different agitations and temptations of the enemy in order to try him." We shall have to explore more fully in the next section that phrase, "in order to try him," since Ignatius discusses in the important ninth rule the various possible reasons why God permits the evil spirit to work on us in desolation. For the moment, though, his point is that God's grace and help is always present to every soul, even though we may not feel his presence.

It is an article of faith that God always gives us, for as long as we live, "sufficient grace for eternal salvation" (#320). But in desolation we easily doubt this, just as we easily forget that desolation never lasts forever. When our feelings are disturbed, we quickly lose sight of the fundamental truths of revelation which ground our hope in the Lord. The evil spirit seeks to flood and paralyze our understanding by means of our desolate feelings. And we must work against him here too. Just as we must *act* in a way opposite to his inspirations, so too must we hold tenaciously to the *thoughts* of faith and hope which contradict his diabolical thoughts of doubt and despair.[4]

Why the Lord Permits Desolation

St. Ignatius' advice as to how we should act and think in desolation makes clear that desolation is never from God; it is never his "voice," never caused by him. Yet when the devout soul is overtaken by feelings of turmoil, sadness or frustration, the normal reaction is to ask: "What is God saying to me? Is he displeased with my life? Have I somehow offended him?" If the soul is submissive, she will struggle to accept the misery she experiences as "God's will." It would seem, however, that our whole discussion above calls into question this pious acceptance of desolation. If it is never from God, never caused by him, is the soul mistaken in accepting it as his "will" for her?

The answer is "yes and no." Usually such a reaction does represent a misunderstanding of the way God is working in our lives, an echo of the puppeteer God, or the Father of small children, which we found in early Old Testament religion. There is at least a hint of this in St. Teresa's complaint that it is no

---

4 St. Ignatius returns to this point in rules 10 and 11 (#323-324), where he gives the only guidelines for consolation to appear in these first week rules. His point is merely to show that consolation and desolation, being opposites, require opposite responses on the part of the soul. Since consolation and desolation alternate as surely as do night and day, one in consolation should "consider how he will conduct himself during the time of ensuing desolation, and store up a supply of strength as defense against that day" (#323). And whereas in desolation we must renew our hope and reaffirm our faith, in consolation one should "humble himself . . . as much as possible. Let him recall how little he is able to do in desolation, when he is left without such grace or consolation" (#324). In both desolation and consolation, we should work against being carried away by our feelings. Our reason can provide a healthy, sober balance in the face of their possible excesses.

wonder the Lord has so few friends, considering the way he treats the few he does have.

There is, however, also a grain of truth in the devout soul's reaction. In some sense, desolation must come from God, since nothing can happen which is beyond his providence and control. To use a distinction which I have found crucial in directing good souls, while the Lord can never *cause* desolation, it cannot happen unless he *permits* it. The same is true, of course, of sin: It is impossible that the all-holy God causes sin or temptation, since even the suggestion of evil would contradict his absolute goodness. But neither sin nor temptation could ever occur unless he allowed it. If we said they were totally beyond his control, he would no longer be the sovereign Lord of his creation. We would be in the world of Manichaean dualism — two independent divine forces, one good and the other evil — which St. Augustine was ensnared by at the time of his conversion. In order to come to Christ, Augustine had to reject the idea of an autonomous, sovereign evil deity. The devil, as he saw, is truly malevolent, but he is a creature ultimately subject to his Creator.

How, then, can a good God permit evil (and desolation is an evil)? Granted that he does not cause it, why does he not prevent it? Since he is Lord even of evil men and evil spirits, would his goodness not demand that he intervene to prevent their abuses? That is the problem to which St. Ignatius addresses himself, with specific reference to the evil of desolation, in the important ninth rule of the first week. He says there that there are three distinct reasons why the good God might permit desolation in the lives of committed souls.

Before considering Ignatius' three reasons, let us recall that the classic statement of the problem of desolation, and its solution, was already formulated about 400 years before the time of Jesus by the great author of the Book of Job. At the beginning of chapter 2, we discussed the contrasting images of God revealed in the debate between Job and his "friends"; the puppeteer God versus the Father of adult sons and daughters. The unknown author of this story clearly identifies with Job in the debate. And early in the book he reveals his own understanding — the revealed understanding — of how Job came to be in his sad situation to begin with.

One day the Sons of God came to attend on Yahweh, and among them was Satan. So Yahweh said to Satan, "Where have you been?" "Round the earth," he answered "roaming about." So Yahweh asked him, "Did you notice my servant Job? There is no one like him on the earth; a sound and honest man who fears God and shuns evil." "Yes," Satan said "but Job is not God-fearing for nothing, is he? Have you not put a wall round him and his house and all his domain? You have blessed all he undertakes, and his flocks throng the countryside. But stretch out your hand and lay a finger on his possessions: I'll warrant you, he will curse you to your face." "Very well," Yahweh said to Satan "all that he has is in your power. But keep your hand off his person" (Job 1:6-12).

Satan, with the permission of the Lord God, then went forth to strike Job's livestock, his servants, even his children. And when these tragedies failed to shake Job's trust, Satan returned to ask the Lord for permission to touch his person:

"Skin for skin! . . . A man will give away all he has to save his life. But stretch out your hand and lay a finger on his bone and flesh; I warrant you, he will curse you to your face." "Very well," Yahweh said to Satan, "he is in your power. But spare his life" (Job 2:4-6).

Satan did his best — or his worst — but Job stood fast in his trust, as we all know. The important insight for our purposes is that *Satan* is the cause of Job's desolating experiences, though he cannot act without God's permission. And why does God permit Satan to try Job so severely? In some mysterious way, it is to test or prove Job's love and fidelity. Of this the author of the Book of Job is certain. It is true that he cannot fully resolve for us the mystery of God's permitting evil. The book ends with a call to simple trust: The good Lord who created the heavens and the earth and all that is in them, who has "given orders to the morning or sent the dawn to its post" (Job 38:12), cannot possibly be the cause of evil, of desolation. But, by the same reasoning, neither can these events and experiences be beyond his control.

Thus the good God permits but does not cause the desolation in Job's life and ours. Why does he allow it? The author of Job can only tell us that, in some obscure way, it "proves" Job's love and fidelity. When St. Ignatius confronts the same question in rule 9 of week one, he is able, with the guidance of the Holy Spirit, to lift further the veil of mystery surrounding the problem of evil in the lives of committed souls. There are, he tells us, three possible reasons why God may permit the evil spirit to cause them to experience desolation:

> The principal reasons why we suffer from desolation are three: The first is because we have been tepid and slothful or negligent in our exercises of piety, and so through our own fault spiritual consolation has been taken away from us. The second reason is because God wishes to try us, to see how much we are worth, and how much we will advance in his service and praise when left without the generous reward of consolations and signal favors. The third reason is because God wishes to give us a true knowledge and understanding of ourselves, so that we may have an intimate perception of the fact that it is not within our power to acquire and attain great devotion, intense love, tears or any other spiritual consolation; but that all this is the gift and grace of God our Lord (#322).

The three possible reasons for desolation, then, are our own negligence, God's desire to "test" our love, and his wish to teach us that genuine consolation is pure gift, that we cannot manipulate or control its bestowal. It is important to note that only one of these three reasons—the first—refers to our own negligence. Most devout souls, when they experience desolation, immediately infer that they must have displeased God in some way, that it is their own fault that the Lord seems far away. This is indeed one possibility, but it is not the only one.

When souls come to me in desolation, I always point this out to them. The more seriously they take their relationship to God the more likely they are to feel that the desolation they experience is a sign of their own negligence, that in some way God is displeased with them. Even if this is true, the desolation is not intended to "punish" them but to wake them up to the fact they have drifted from their earlier fervor. Recall that we presuppose in these rules that we are dealing with generous, committed men and women to whom God is important. Such people can and do drift, even unconsciously. The pressure of work can lead them to neglect their prayer; or friendships can enter their lives which gradually compromise their total commitment to the Lord; or they can imperceptibly absorb the "worldly" values of the secular milieu within which they live and work. In all these cases and others like them the Lord may permit the devil to do his desolating work; but while the devil's goal is to destroy the person, the Lord's intent is to shock them into realizing their negligence, and to restore them to their earlier fervor.

Sometimes, though, good people will say, "I can't see how I have been negligent. When I examine my life it seems to me I fail in many ways, but I failed in the same ways in the past and then God seemed very close." If this is true, or if we cannot discover any deliberate negligence which might explain our desolation, then we can be quite sure negligence or sloth or tepidity is not the reason for it. "But," such persons may say, "perhaps I have displeased the Lord in some way which I do not realize." If they do say this, I always insist that such doubts or fears should not be taken seriously. The Lord is more desirous of our sanctification than we are. He is not playing guessing games with us or tormenting us by leaving us to twist slowly in the wind. Such a God is no God at all. Thus we should say to him in this situation: "Lord, you know I desire only to please you. You are free to correct me in any way you wish. But I cannot see where I have grown negligent or tepid, despite my sincere efforts to examine my conscience. So please make it clear to me if I am somehow failing you. Unless or until you do, I will not take seriously these vague doubts and anxieties."

Such a prayer pleases him immensely: Far from being presumptuous, it is a strong affirmation of our trust in his goodness. And there are, as St. Ignatius tells us, two other reasons besides our negligence why God might permit us to experience desolation. If we cannot pinpoint any specific negligence as its cause, we should look to these other reasons. They explain why even fervent and committed souls experience desolation.

In the first place, Ignatius says we may experience desolation because the Lord desires thereby to teach us "that it is not within our power to acquire and attain . . . spiritual consolation; but that all this is the gift and grace of God our Lord."[5] That is, he wishes to teach us that everything is gift, especially our experience of him in consolation. There are no techniques for producing the experience of God.[6] He is the Lord of the encounter, and he comes and goes as *he* sees best. In theory we know this; but in practice we all seek to manipulate our encounters with him. We want him to come when we desire him. We try the latest prayer techniques and follow the fashionable gurus of the moment in the hope of finding the magic key to his heart. When we find a place or posture or mantra which brings consolation, we return to it again and again in the hope that we can recapture the experience of God. What is God's response to all this? Desolation! If we are lucky, our efforts to control the encounter will not work. Like the fox in *The Little Prince*, our God is "timid" and flees from those who seek to grasp him or to move too close too quickly. This is painful for the ardent soul to discover, but it has to be this way. Otherwise, God would not be God. If we could produce him at will — if consolation were to be had by our own techniques and devices — then he would not really be God, but the figment of our imagination and emotions. As Ignatius goes on to say, "God does not wish us to build on the property of another, to rise up in spirit in a certain pride and vainglory and attribute to ourselves the devotion and other effects of spiritual consolation."

There is another, more mysterious reason given by Ignatius to explain why even fervent souls experience desolation. He says it is "because God wishes to try us, to see how much we will advance in his service and praise when left without the generous reward of consolations and signal favors." For many years this reason puzzled and confused me. Taken literally, it seemed to make no sense. Why would God need to "try" us — literally, to test us — since he knows everything? Surely he knows what we are made of and what we can do when left to our own resources. Nothing is concealed from his wisdom.

As I puzzled over this, my own experience as a teacher

---

5 This is Ignatius' third reason in #322. For purposes that will soon be clear, I have inverted the order of discussion of his second and third reasons.

6 We stressed this matter in *Opening to God*, ch. 1 and 4.

gradually suggested a possible answer to me. Occasionally I have a student in one of my courses who is "over his head" in the subject matter. It becomes clear to me that he can't possibly pass the course, barring a miracle. Since many of the students take my courses as electives, they can drop my subject and replace it by another without jeopardizing their graduation. And so I try to persuade such a student that it would be better to drop the course while there is still time, rather than have a failing grade on his permanent record. Sometimes the student sees my point and accepts the advice gratefully; but some weak students are not very realistic about their limits and insist that they can make it, that the next exam will be better, that they are just "getting adjusted" to my style of teaching and my demands. In such a case, I find it best to allow the student to take the next exam, not because I think he can pass it but because *he* thinks so. I hope to help him to discover and accept what I already know: that the course is too demanding for him and it would be for his own good to drop it. When he fails again I am not surprised or enlightened, but maybe he is.

Could desolation be a "test" in this sense, intended not to show God himself but to show *us* our limitations "when left without the generous reward of consolations and signal favors"? For some time I thought this might be what St. Ignatius meant; it certainly is true that desolation has this purpose in our lives. The problem, however, as I gradually came to realize, is that this is precisely the point of the *preceding* reason which we discussed: By means of desolation, God brings us to realize that everything is gift and that we cannot merit or produce his love or his consolation. Could Ignatius merely be making the same point twice in these two reasons? That seemed very unlikely to me. St. Ignatius is a man of very few words, and those few were prayed over and chiseled for many years. It is hard to imagine that such a man would repeat himself in this way.

But what then is the meaning of "test" here? What distinct point is he making concerning the Lord's reasons for allowing the evil spirit to test us by desolation? I think perhaps we have a clue in the phrase "testing steel by fire." Steel is an alloy of carbon and iron, and the process of refining and purifying the alloy or combination is called "testing." To test the steel is to subject it to intense heat, thereby fusing the carbon and iron into a new, purer and much stronger substance than the original ingredients. This, I believe, is an analogy for Ignatius' second reason why God permits devout souls to experience desolation. This desolation is the purifying fire in which our love is made strong and perfect. It "burns out" of our love all the impurities of selfishness and timidity, and it "fuses" the soul to the Spirit of Jesus. If our life were all consolation, we would be soft and weak in our love.

As we noted earlier, marriage is "for better or worse." When young couples marry, they think this means — and it does mean to them — "I hope it will always be 'better,' but if the 'worse' comes I will try to persevere." But that is not really the meaning of the phrase, as those who have lived long in marriage come to realize. We need the "worse" just as much as the "better," strange as that may sound to an age of sentimentalized love. In the better we learn the joy of loving; and in the worse we learn to love unselfishly. The worse is the fire which purifies our love of all the self-seeking which is in each of us. It is when misunderstandings arise in a marriage, when one person feels betrayed or disappointed by the other, that the real strength of love emerges. If a woman remains loyal to her man even when things are difficult between them, then she can be sure she really loves him for himself, "for better or worse," and not merely for what she gets out of him. Similarly, desolation is the "worse" of our love relationship with God. It both reveals and strengthens our love; it "tests" that love in a purifying and transforming fire.[7]

Like a Woman, a False Lover, a Military Commander

The soul who understands the reason for his or her experience of desolation will be much better able to cope with the experience. If she has been negligent, she can discover the cure for desolation in a change of her lifestyle and a return to fidelity.

---

7 In *A Commentary on Saint Ignatius' Rules for the Discernment of Spirits,* Jules Toner has a fine discussion of the three Ignatian reasons for desolation (pp. 182-191). While I have inverted the order of the second and third reasons in order to clarify the meaning of the second, Toner treats them in the order given by St. Ignatius. He also suggests some other possible reasons why the Lord might permit desolation (p. 191).

If, on the other hand, she cannot discover any serious negligence in her life to explain the darkness and turmoil she experiences, then she can be reassured to know that desolation comes even to fervent souls. She can submit gracefully, if not gratefully, to the purifying fire which "tests" her love, and she can learn the lesson that all is gift and deepen her humble, trustful dependence on the giver of every gift. Usually, at least in my experience, these two "positive" reasons — the "testing" and the "letting go" — are *both* applicable when desolation comes in the life of a faithful friend of the Lord. It is not a question of determining which of these two purposes the Lord has, but of seeing desolation as the instrument for accomplishing both of them at once.

This, of course, is the purpose of the Lord who permits desolation. The devil who causes it has entirely different ends in view. He hopes to discourage and defeat the soul, to turn it aside from its generous beginnings. Unfortunately for us, he is a treacherous and subtle adversary, oftentimes much more successful than he was with Job. And so St. Ignatius, who himself was brought to the brink of suicide by the deceits of Satan, ends his rules for the first week with three famous analogies whereby he seeks to unmask the character and tactics of the devil: "The enemy conducts himself as a woman. . . . Our enemy may also be compared in his manner of acting to a false lover. . . . The conduct of our enemy may also be compared to the tactics of a (military) leader" (#325-327). Each of the three brings out one important characteristic of the evil spirit's way with men and women.

Like a woman. This is a dangerous comparison to use in our feminist age. But Ignatius clearly does not mean *every* woman here. Nor, I think, *only* women. He says that, like a woman, the devil "is a weakling before a show of strength, and a tyrant if he has his will." The point, I take it, is that a woman generally cannot rely on physical strength, on brute force, to get her way. Men can often do that, although it is wrong. But women, and men who are physically weaker, have to rely on their wits — by nagging, screaming, sobbing, threatening and, in general, psychological warfare — to tyrannize or outwit others. If we accept that contrast, and I feel it is as true today as when Ignatius wrote, then his point is that Satan cannot overcome those who belong to Jesus Christ by brute force. He has to depend on threats and subtle pressures and, like a physically weaker but nagging person, is ruthless when we are timid and cowardly when we are firm.

> The enemy becomes weak, loses courage, and turns to flight with his seductions as soon as one leading a spiritual life faces his temptations boldly, and does exactly the opposite of what he suggests. However, if one begins to be afraid and to lose courage in temptations, no wild animal on earth can be more fierce than the enemy of our human nature (#325).

Are all women like this? Thank God, no! But I think I know by experience that such women (and men) do exist. Similarly, when Ignatius next compares the devil to a false lover, he does not imply that all men are false lovers. But some are; and such a lover "seeks to remain hidden and does not want to be discovered." When he (or she) seeks to seduce another, "he wants his words and solicitations kept secret" (#326). The false lover will persuade the girl not to tell her father or brothers, since they are old-fashioned and narrow-minded. Similarly, the devil will urge the soul not to confide in a confessor or a director or a superior; they are too busy, too strict, too lax, too modern or too old-fashioned. "For he knows that he cannot succeed in his evil undertaking, once his evident deceits have been revealed."

Finally, the enemy is like a military commander. A good army leader reconnoiters and plans. He studies the whole situation, and probes to discover the physical and psychological weaknesses of his adversary. Then he attacks "at the weakest point." No successful commander attacks where his enemy is strongest. Nor does our angelic enemy. He studies our character and searches for our Achilles' heel. If we are naturally timid, he seeks to make us cowardly; if we are prone to vanity, he feeds our ego with flattery; if we are sentimental, he encourages an emotionalistic piety which is all froth and no substance. How important it is, then, that we know ourselves and our own weaknesses. Once we know them, we can bring them to the Lord for healing, and the devil's advantage will be lost.

Such is the enemy of our human nature: a deceitful bully who loves secrecy and works in the dark, and a crafty tactician who is cleverer than we are. Fortunately, though, he is not at war with us alone. His real adversary is Jesus Christ, to whom we belong. We can abandon the Lord. But as long as we cling to him, even the evil spirit's deceits are the means for our sanctification. "For those who love God, all things work together unto good" (Rom 8:28). Even desolation!

Practicum Questions

1. We have seen three reasons why God permits us to experience desolation. Which of the three would you think applied to the experience of Job?

2. Recall an important experience of desolation in your own life. In the light of our discussion in this chapter (of the rules and of the devil's wiles) how well did you interpret and cope with the experience?

Part III
A Mixed
Harvest

Chapter 7
Commitment and Consolation

When the evil spirit, the enemy of our human nature, sets his mind to accomplishing our downfall, he is not easily discouraged. Thus the beginner in the life of grace is not home free once he or she has learned to cope with the trials of desolation. An important victory has indeed been won, and the soul will not readily be deceived by the same tactics in the future. But if he is anything, the devil is shrewd. Desolations will come; they are, in fact, as normal a part of human life as are rainy days. And the devil will use them as an ongoing "probing operation," continually testing for signs of vulnerability in the soul's armor. This will be especially true when new challenges arise. As we noted in chapter 6, our "yes" to the Lord is not a once and for all thing. At any moment we say yes to the Lord's present call to us, but he reveals his will gradually and there are always new "beginnings," calls to a deeper level of commitment. The soul is again challenged to launch farther into the deep.

As St. John of the Cross says in discussing the dark night of the soul (perhaps the most crucial of these new beginnings in the interior life), many souls enter the night — or nights, since there are several — but very few persevere till the end of the journey. Why is this? It is not because such souls are bad; they are, in fact, good and sincere pray-ers. Otherwise they would never have come into the dark night. But these new beginnings present new challenges, and the evil spirit again returns to the attack. Fears about my own resources, self-pity, anxiety concerning the "dehumanizing" cost of journeying onward — all forms of desolation — lead good and committed pray-ers to settle for a comfortable mediocrity in their relationship with the Lord. Unless they are courageous and open to the challenge of a good spiritual director, they will buy peace with the devil by abandoning their dreams to love as they are loved. The same thing happens, of course, in most human relationships: As the cost of loving escalates, many of us grow weary and settle for much less than we had dreamed of. How many marriages (or religious vocations) do we see that realize in maturity the full promise of courtship days?[1] It is not that people are bad. Most are good, but their goodness and generosity have limits. And, as we said, the devil is shrewd: He probes and tests by means of desolation until he finds those limits, and then he exploits them fully. His shrewdness, however, is not manifested only by these probing bouts of desolation. He also is able to mask himself as an angel of light and to use consolation to block the soul's growth. With committed souls, his end is one and the same, whether he works by desolation or by pseudoconsolation. Ultimately, of course, this end is to bring souls to his kingdom and to enlist them under his battle standard. But more immediately he seeks, with committed men and women, to block their growth and persuade them to settle for that comfortable mediocrity of which we spoke: The present good becomes the enemy of the divine better.

The Ambiguity of Consolation

In speaking of desolation in chapter 6, we said that, for souls whose fundamental option is for God, desolation is *never* his voice. He does permit it, for reasons which we have seen, but he never causes it. Thus the pray-er should never make or change a faith decision in times of desolation, since to do so would be to have the devil for his spiritual director.

1 Father Jules Toner (*op. cit.*, Appendix II, pp. 271-282) has a fruitful comparison of Ignatian desolation with St. John of the Cross' dark nights. He concludes that they differ in essential ways, primarily because Ignatian desolation is caused by the evil spirit, whereas the "dark night" is really caused by the presence of the all-holy God to the still sinful soul. I have taken a different approach here (and in chapters 4 and 5 of *When the Well Runs Dry*), since I believe the dark night of John is desolation not *because* of the painful presence of the Living Flame of Love to the untransformed soul but because the devil and self-pity insinuate themselves and take advantage of the soul's vulnerability. Thus, in my opinion, the misery of the dark night would be the instance, *par excellence*, of Ignatian desolation. This would also explain why I said in the *Well* that the soul can become at home in the dark, at peace with the pain, in which case the dark night would no longer be desolation!

It would be natural to assume, then, that consolation — since it is the opposite of desolation — would always be God's voice, and that the soul can safely follow inspirations which come at times of consolation. Unfortunately, this is not true. If it were, the job of spiritual direction (as well as the work of discernment) would be easy enough. It is true, as St. Ignatius has said in the first week rules (#315), that for committed souls "it is characteristic of the evil spirit to harass with anxiety, to afflict with sadness, to raise obstacles backed by fallacious reasonings that disturb the soul . . . (whereas) it is characteristic of the good spirit to give courage and strength, consolations, tears, inspirations, and peace." These are the *characteristic* ways of acting of each of the spirits warring for the soul's allegiance. Moreover, since God is truth and goodness and can never act contrary to his nature, desolation, while painful, is relatively easy to discern. We can be sure, given the Lord's fidelity and truthfulness, that it is never from him.

The problem, however, is that the evil spirit is the father of lies. His shrewdness is unprincipled and thus he has no scruples about mimicking the voice of God when it suits his purposes. When he cannot deceive or block the committed soul by means of desolation, he seeks to imitate the Lord's way of speaking and acting. Thus it is that consolation, which properly belongs to the arsenal of the good spirit, becomes a prime weapon of his adversary, the evil spirit. This is why St. Ignatius, when he repeats the general norm for consolation and desolation in the first rule of the second week, adds one crucial word to his descriptions:

> It is characteristic of God and his angels, when they act upon the soul, to give *true* happiness and spiritual joy, and to banish all the sadness and disturbances which are caused by the enemy. It is characteristic of the evil one to fight against such happiness and consolation by proposing fallacious reasonings, subtleties and continual deceptions (#329).

We are familiar with this general norm from the first week rules (and chapter 5 above); the crucial word added, though, is "true." *True* consolation can only come from God.

No such qualification is attached to desolation. Ignatius does not speak of true desolation as from the evil spirit. Nor does he need to. In a perverse way, all desolation is true desolation, since the good God, ever true to his own being and nature, could never mimic the voice of his satanic adversary. When we turn to consolation, however, deceit is possible; and so we must distinguish between true and false consolation, between that which is really from God and that which only appears to be from him. This distinction, in fact, is the central purpose of the rules of the second week. Since consolation can be from either the good or the evil spirit, how do we determine in concrete situations which spirit is inspiring us to act?

St. Ignatius' rules for this ambiguous situation presuppose and affirm one essential, consoling truth: However wily and deceitful the evil spirit may be, he can never perfectly mimic the consolations of God. He can produce ecstasies and visions; and he can foster, for his own ends, the noblest of humanitarian projects and the most intense apostolic zeal, but the tail of the snake will always appear when the devil is in the picture.[2]

For those with eyes to see and experience of his ways, the evil spirit's fingerprints will always mar his cleverest forgeries. The second week rules of St. Ignatius are our best guidelines for detecting these forgeries.

Consolation Without Previous Cause

There is one type of consolation which the devil cannot simulate. St. Ignatius calls it "without any previous cause" and discusses it in the second rule of the second week (#330), immediately following the general norm discussed above. With the exception of a very important cautionary note at the end of the rules (#336: rule 8), this is the only mention he makes of this special experience of consolation. Despite, or perhaps because of, Ignatius' lapidary brevity here, the great Karl Rahner has seen this unique and infallible experience of consolation as the core of the *Spiritual Exercises*. Hence this rule and its interpretation have

---

2 Recall our discussion in chapter 5 of what we mean here by the "devil" or the evil spirit. While simplicity and clarity seem best served by referring to the devil as he (or she) throughout, all that we say can equally well be applied to *whatever* forces are working against God in our lives; our own deep-rooted self-love (the "flesh") and the secular, materialistic values of our culture (the "world"), as well as the literal devil.

commanded much attention in recent literature on discernment.[3] While the discussion, however, like any initiated by Karl Rahner, has great speculative theological interest, I do not believe it bears much on the actual *practice* of direction and discernment. First, though, let us hear St. Ignatius speak for himself.

Rule 2 (#330) reads as follows:

> God alone can give consolation to the soul without any previous cause. It belongs solely to the Creator to come into a soul, to leave it, to act upon it, to draw it wholly to the love of his Divine Majesty. I said without previous cause, that is, without any preceding perception or knowledge of any subject by which a soul might be led to such a consolation through its own acts of intellect and will.

The distinctive note of this experience of consolation is that it is "without any previous cause." By contrast, as Ignatius says in rule 3, "if a cause precedes," the consolation in question can come either from the "good angel" or the evil spirit. It is, then, the "uncaused" character of this consolation that marks it as surely from God.

What does it mean to say consolation is without previous cause? Ignatius explains, at the end of rule 2, that he means "without any preceding perception or knowledge of any subject" which might lead the soul to experience consolation "through its own acts of intellect and will." A cause then would be some "preceding perception or knowledge." For example, a beautiful sunset which leads me to wonder at the goodness of the Creator. Or the recollection (or the presence) of someone I love, as a result of which I am filled with gratitude to God for the gift of friendship. The wonder, the gratitude are consolations — spiritual consolations — since God is their object. And the "cause" is the sensible experience of a sunset or the sensible memory of a friend.

---

3 Toner, (*op. cit.*, Appendix IV, pp. 291-313) has what I consider an excellent discussion of this celebrated controversy. Based on my own experience as a pray-er and a director of pray-ers, I would agree with his conclusions that (a) this consolation "without cause" is relatively rare (though perhaps not as rare as Toner implies) in the life of prayer; and thus (b) that Ignatius did *not* intend to make it, *pace* Rahner, the "basic question" in the logic and practice of discernment. The latter conclusion is perhaps confirmed by the fact that Ignatius devotes four rules to consolation "with cause," as against this single reference to that "without cause."

Similarly, my favorite scripture passage, a loved hymn, or the praise of a superior could all be preceding causes. Anything in the senses which leads me, through the mediation of my "own acts of intellect and will" (that is, through attention to, reflection upon, and response to the sensible experience), to a consoling experience of God and his love would be a preceding cause in St. Ignatius' sense.

If my understanding of "preceding cause" is correct, it would seem that most of our religious experiences would have a preceding cause in the senses. Specifically, when we meditate upon a scriptural passage or imaginatively contemplate a biblical scene, the resultant consolation would be caused by our pious thoughts or images. As we shall see shortly, such consolations are not bad or false; but since they do involve the senses and the imagination, they have to be discerned carefully. As St. John of the Cross tells us, both the Lord and the evil spirit can work through the senses. Nonetheless, naturally speaking, as the scholastic philosophers have always taught, all of our knowledge comes through the senses. To reject such experiences out of hand, even in the sphere of religious experience, would amount to intellectual and emotional starvation.

What, then, does Ignatius mean by consolation "without preceding cause"? Since it is consolation, it is joy, peace, an increase in faith, in hope and in love. Yet it comes to us without sensible cause, without the thoughts and images which usually trigger such a consoling experience of peace. This may be hard to imagine — and rightly so. We are creatures of sense and not angels. For this reason, it seems clear to me that such a non-sense experience of God could scarcely be the normal, or even the ideal, experience for us human beings. I don't believe that this could be the core experience of those *Spiritual Exercises* which St. Ignatius composed primarily for beginners in the interior life, exercises which lay heavy stress on the preceding causes of meditative reflection and imaginative contemplation.

Still in all, Ignatius clearly believes that consolations "without (sensible) cause" do occur. They are, indeed, very special and precious since they alone are infallibly from God: "God alone can give consolation to the soul without any previous cause." Inspirations to act which came at such a time—during such a consolation—could only be from the Lord. But can we give any examples of such sure consolations? While Ignatius does not offer any, I believe we can describe two situations which could qualify as consolation without any previous cause.

First, imagine a situation in which a devout and generous person is misunderstood and criticized. Despite her good intentions, her religious superior or her peers misread her motives or criticize her work. This is painful to any normal human being. And so the soul in question feels hurt and frustrated. Moreover, being sincere and devout, she begins to wonder if maybe she is deceived and deceiving others. And so goes before the Lord in the tabernacle in a state of misery and distress—of desolation. There are sensible causes for her feelings, but these are all causes apt to produce (as they do) not consolation but desolation. And yet, as she kneels helplessly and almost hopelessly before her Lord, suddenly she seems to hear him saying interiorly: "You came to this life for me and not for these people. All that matters is what I think of you." And she is very much at peace in the midst of the pain. She was not meditating on why she came or giving herself a pious sermon (which would be a preceding cause); the realization and the peace simply came together, as if "out of the blue." And the depth of peace she feels may very well coexist with continued surface pain in the feelings.

The above experience occurs, I believe, in the lives of virtually all devout souls. The fact that the "darkness in the marketplace" is an integral part of our interior transformation would almost guarantee that there would be such experiences. Furthermore, the consolation described seems to be without sensible cause. There are many "causes" operative in the senses and faculties of such a person, but they would all tend to cause not consolation but desolation. There seems to be no preceding cause for the "out of the blue" experience of consolation.

A second example of a consolation without preceding cause might be the following: suppose a faithful pray-er has been living the experience of the dry well at prayer. There is not turmoil or anxiety, since the person has become accustomed to this dryness as his normal mode of prayer. God seems very silent, meditation and imaginative contemplation are useless or impossible, and the head is empty, except for myriad distractions which float in and out and seem to lead nowhere. Much of the time the pray-er scarcely adverts to them. Yet, deep down he is at peace. There seems no sensible reason for it—nothing tangible that he can lay hold of—and yet there is a real peace in the blackness. That too, I believe, is an example of consolation without sensible cause. And, as the pray-er matures, it may be a fairly common state, much more common than the "consolation wrapped in sensible desolation" which we described above.

The reader may be able to suggest other instances of such consolation without preceding cause. In any event, the important fact is that such can happen and that they are *surely* from God. He alone, as St. John of the Cross tells us, can work directly on the soul without the mediation of the senses. Even in such experiences, though, St. Ignatius adds an important cautionary note. While inspirations to act which come at such a time can only be from God, we must, he says (#336: rule 8), "consider it very attentively, and must cautiously distinguish the actual time of the consolation from the period which follows it. At such a time the soul is still fervent and favored with the grace and aftereffects of the consolation which has passed." We might describe this as an "afterglow," a lingering peace and joy which remains in the soul even after the Spirit of God has passed by. It is, I believe, a quite normal experience in the life of devout pray-ers. And while beautiful, it is also, as Ignatius tells us, somewhat dangerous. At such a time

> the soul frequently forms various resolutions and plans which are not granted directly by God our Lord. They may come from our own reasoning on the relations of our concepts and on the consequences of our judgments, or they may come from the good or evil spirit. Hence they (these resolutions and plans) must be carefully examined before they are given full approval and put into execution.

It seems, then, that when we speak of consolation without cause we must distinguish the actual time of such a consolation from its afterglow. The consolation itself can only be from God, and any inspiration to act which comes at such a time is surely his voice. But the dividing line between such an experience and its afterglow is a fine one. I have found the following analogy helpful in clarifying the point St. Ignatius is making. Imagine a glider plane being towed by a jet. While the two are joined together the glider can fly very high and reach enormous speeds, even though it has no power supply of its own. But once the rope or chain linking it to the jet is severed, the glider will inevitably return to earth. Its descent, however, will be very gradual and, if the glider pilot is skilled, he can cruise for a long time on the momentum acquired while he was being towed by the jet. During this long glide, an inexperienced onlooker or passenger might believe the glider to be flying on its own power, or somehow to be still drawn by the jet despite the fact the chain has been severed.

The situation is similar in consolation without cause. God is the jet plane and we are the glider. When we are held to him in the close embrace of consolation, we can fly very high and reach enormous speeds, not by our own power but by his. Once, however, the cord of consolation is cut, we lose our power supply. Consolation, as we saw in chapter 6, is pure gift and not within our power to produce or prolong. But like the glider we don't normally crash to the earth in an instant. The acquired momentum, or the afterglow, of the consolation carries us for some time. This time, Ignatius says, is a dangerous one. The soul is no longer in the embrace of God, and yet it seems to be flying high. It is, quite literally, back to its senses, dependent on its own natural reasoning and imagination and thus also, as we shall see shortly, vulnerable again to the pious deceits of the evil spirit. The special danger arises because the glider, soaring high above the earth, may not realize that it has been severed from the jet. It may, and often does, take its inspirations and insights as still coming directly from the divine jet.

Thus, while consolation without sensible cause is a sure and precious experience of God and can be a valuable guide to discern his will, it is not the normal experience of human beings. Nor can it be followed without great care and sound direction. Furthermore, it seems to me that a good director could never give automatic credence to a pray-er's report of such an experience.

Why? Because the consolation in question is, by its very nature, deeply interior and non-sensible. The director cannot enter into the pray-er's soul; he or she can only judge by the visible, tangible fruits of the experience. From these fruits the director can judge (and I often have judged) that a particular experience was "consolation without cause"; but without evidence of these fruits there would be no basis for a sound judgment.

Consolation With Preceding Cause

The period of afterglow which makes consolation without cause particularly tricky to discern is a time when our own reasoning and imagination become quite active: We seek to cling to the Lord and prolong the experience; we begin to ask what return we can make to him for his great love, and how we can share the experience with others. These reflections and desires can prolong our devotion, but note it is now of quite a different nature. It has a sensible cause, namely, our own reflections and imaginings. In this sense it becomes like most of the consolations we experience, particularly as beginners. As we have seen, the normal way to encounter God is via our own reasoning and imagining, through the use of our own natural faculties.

Is this bad? Not at all. It is, as we have said, the normal way to God; moreover, the *Spiritual Exercises* are intended precisely as ways to employ these faculties in the search for God and his will. To meditate or to contemplate (in the Ignatian sense) is precisely to seek God in this way. Hence I find it mistaken and misleading when a pray-er says to me, "Is this consolation from God or is it just my own imagination?" That is a false dichotomy. If we are to believe St. Ignatius (or St. Teresa of Avila, for that matter), God normally and for much of our lives works precisely through our imagination and understanding, and our senses. The real question is: Whether in a "supernatural" manner or by means of our natural faculties, is God the one working, speaking to me, or not? Are my thoughts and images, and the consolations they produce, from him or from some other, deceitful spirit? In the case of consolations "with preceding cause," either may be true. As St. Ignatius says, "If a cause precedes, both the good angel and the evil spirit can give consolation to a soul, but for a quite different purpose" (#331: rule 3).

That God would seek to lead the soul to grow in love and generosity by means of consolation seems quite evident. But why would the evil spirit give the soul peace, joy and love, or at least seek to counterfeit these gifts? In the following rule St. Ignatius tells us:

It is a mark of the evil spirit to assume the appearance of an angel of light. He begins by suggesting thoughts that are suited to a devout soul, and ends by suggesting his own. For example, he will suggest holy and pious thoughts that are wholly in conformity with the sanctity of the soul. Afterwards, he will endeavor little by little to end by drawing the soul into his hidden snares and evil designs (#332).

Recall that we are considering a devout soul, for whom enticements to what is obviously evil would have little attraction. Furthermore, the soul in question is relatively mature and stable in her commitment to the Lord. She is no longer the "beginner" of the first week of the *Spiritual Exercises*, whom the evil spirit can hope to turn away from her commitment by discouragement, fear, anxiety or other forms of desolation. In order to deceive her now, he has to come to her under the appearance of good. He has to use her very desire for God and holiness as a means to lead her astray. If she loves to pray, he will encourage this love (and even reward her with visions and revelations and other unusual experiences) in order to foster pride or to cause her to neglect her apostolic responsibilities. If she has found new life in a charismatic prayer community, he will encourage dependence on this community in a way that leads to exclusivity and a pharisaical disdain for "outsiders." If she is generously committed to the works of justice and charity, he will foster this commitment to the point where "mediocre" church leaders are despised and prayer seems an irrelevant luxury.

These are just examples—common enough but by no means the only ones—of the ways the enemy of our human nature can sow his weeds in the wheat field of God. As long as we live he will be working to spoil the harvest of sanctity in good souls. In fact, one of the surest signs of interior maturity which I have found is a healthy mistrust of even our best motivations. St. John of the

Cross tells us that the more we grow in God, and the greater our potential for good in the church, the more the devil will be working to spoil the harvest. It makes sense. After all, if you were the devil, where would you concentrate your efforts? Would it not be on those with the greatest potential for good in the world and in the church? You would not waste much energy on halfhearted or mediocre souls, and even less on those who already belonged to you! This is why our popes and bishops and civil leaders command special attention in our eucharistic prayers.

If our enemy is so treacherous and no pious thought or action is immune to his corruption—even consolation "without preceding cause" being vulnerable in its afterglow—how can we discern the action of God from that of the evil spirit? This is, of course, both the most important and the trickiest aspect of the art of discernment. St. Ignatius treats it in rules 5 and 6 of the second week. In rule 5 he says:

> We must carefully observe the whole course of our thoughts. If the *beginning* and *middle* and *end* . . . are wholly good and directed to what is entirely right, it is a sign that they are from the good angel. But the course of thoughts suggested to us may terminate in something evil, or distracting, or less good than the soul had formerly proposed to do. Again, it may end in what weakens the soul, or disquiets it; or by destroying the peace, tranquillity and quiet which it had before, it may cause disturbance to the soul (#333).

In general, we may say that the devil will always reveal his presence by desolation. He cannot fully mask this presence, nor can he produce a consolation which is genuine throughout. However much he mimics God in the peace and joy of consolation, the tail of the snake will always be evident to those with the eyes to see and the patience to scrutinize their experience. As Ignatius says, "these things (the disquiet, distraction, or deflection to what is less good mentioned above) are a clear sign that the thoughts are proceeding from the evil spirit, the enemy of our progress and eternal salvation."

Nonetheless, it does take keen sight, genuine discernment, to discover the tail of the snake in our consolation experiences. Ignatius says we must examine "the beginning, middle and end" of our consolations; if all three are wholly good, "it is a sign they are from the good angel." If the tail of the snake appears in any of the three—beginning, middle or end—then we should mistrust the whole experience and refuse to be guided by the inspirations which come at such a time. The Ignatian criterion is thus simply stated. But as I and countless other directors and pray-ers have discovered, the practical application of this norm requires years of reflection and experience. Some concrete examples, though, may help to clarify what St. Ignatius means.

The *beginning*. What would it mean to examine the "beginning" of our consolation experience to determine whether it is "wholly good"? I take this beginning to refer to the concrete context of our inspiration to pray. Am I in the right place at the right time for the right reasons? Suppose, for example, that I am strongly drawn to pray when the rest of my religious community is gathering for a community meeting or a common work. Or, as a married man, to leave my family alone several nights a week in order to engage in parish or apostolic work. Again, if I am a student, perhaps a seminarian, to whom God and prayer have only recently become important, suppose that the inspiration to pray comes when I am studying for an important exam the following day or when the seminary time order calls for study. In each case, something is wrong. Prayer is a great good, and God's will is the central concern of any truly committed soul, but it is strange that he should take me away from the demands of obedience and the obligations of my state in life, or even that he should draw me to pray when others will thus have to shoulder my share of the burden of the work. The tail of the snake is already visible (or at least implied) in the *beginning* of such prayer experiences; hence any consolation that follows, or any inspiration to act in a certain way, should be suspect. It is true that Jesus told Martha that Mary had chosen the better part. But we had better be sure that it is really Jesus speaking and calling us in such a situation! He also castigated the Pharisees for a religious correctness and zealous piety which overlooked very real human needs and placed impossible burdens on others.

Could the inspiration to pray, and consequently to act or commit ourselves to a particular course of action, be from the

Lord in such situations? Yes, it could, as many gospel incidents reveal. But such an inspiration could also be from the evil spirit, who enters as an angel of light and seeks to mimic the voice of the Lord. How, then, can we determine who is speaking, in situations where the beginning — the initial inspiration to pray — of the consolation experience is suspect? I find it best simply to tell the Lord (for example, in the case of the seminarian who is strongly drawn to pray when he should be studying), "Lord, if it is really you drawing me, come back at the proper time for prayer. Right now, I am supposed to be studying. That, presumably, is your will for me. If you want something else, it is up to you to make it very clear to me." That may sound like a peculiar way to talk to the Lord, but I am convinced it is what he wants us to do. This is one area where it is definitely better to err on the side of caution, to resist, gently but firmly, any inspiration which is suspect. If it is from the evil spirit, he will soon abandon the temptation. If it is really from the Lord, he can work his way despite our gentle resistance.

The *middle*. When Ignatius speaks of the "middle" of the course of our thoughts, I take it he means what happens during the actual consolation experience itself. Suppose I am in the right place at the right time for the right reasons; this is the proper time for prayer and I come to it with a generous and open heart. And there is consolation in my prayer. If, in such a situation, the devotion which I feel leads to, or is accompanied by vain or judgmental thoughts, then the tail of the snake is manifest in the "middle" of the experience. If I find myself composing the motto for my canonization or resenting or despising those who are less fervent and pious than I am, or *anxious* to cling to God and to reach perfection immediately — if any of these feelings or thoughts are present, then the consolation is not from the Lord, no matter how beautiful (even ecstatic) it may seem.

The other very down-to-earth sign of the evil spirit's presence is this: Suppose I am at prayer and the Lord is very close when someone taps me on the shoulder and tells me I am wanted in the parlor. Or the telephone rings, or the baby starts crying. If I am irate and filled with self-pity ("Can't they even leave me alone for 20 minutes!"), this is a clear sign the consoling prayer, the consolation, was not wholly from the Lord. If it were, I would be surprised at my own serenity and sweetness in accepting the interruption.

It is perhaps important to recall that these "fake" consolations are not a sign that we are bad or insincere. They have happened to me more often than I care to remember; and they are normal in the lives of the best pray-ers I know. As we have said, the devil will always be working, in every possible way, to derail and distract the good. When such things happen, we have to be able to laugh at ourselves and our own instinctive reactions. To be distraught by them would merely be a sign of our own wounded pride, our inability to accept the fact that we are not yet perfect and that the devil can still find our Achilles' heel. At the same time, we should recognize the deceit, and mistrust any consolation (and any consequent inspiration to act or to judge) in which the tail of the snake is thus revealed in the "middle," during the consolation itself.

The *end*. Perhaps the foregoing paragraphs make clear what Ignatius would mean by the "end" of the course of our thoughts. Where does the consolation lead? What are we moved to do or to say or to think as a result of the consolation? This "end" is what Ignatius discusses fully in rule 5 (#333). Does the consolation lead to or "terminate in something evil, or distracting, or less good?" "Does it end in what weakens the soul or disquiets it?" As Ronald Knox has pointed out in his great book, *Enthusiasm*, enthusiastic (intensely devotional) movements in the church have often ended in an idea of "sinless perfection," that is, the conviction that those possessed by the Spirit can no longer sin no matter what they do. Even gross sexual excesses, they believe, are not sinful for those seized by God. Here the "end" of the consolation is clearly evil, and the whole experience bears the marks of the "enemy of our human nature."

Often, though, the end may not be so clearly evil. As Ignatius indicates, it may be merely distracting from, or less good than, my previous commitment to the Lord. Since the lesser good is still a good, the devil's work here is more subtle and harder to discern. The priest committed to and effective in his ministry, who meets and falls in love with Suzibelle, may be convinced that the friendship is good because he now prays much better than he ever did before he met her. Because of her, God is much more real to him. In some sense, this is a good. When he finally decides to leave the ministry to marry Suzibelle, it will be, assuming he is a pious person, because he is convinced that his call is not to many people but to one: He is not abandoning his ministry but merely centering it on the one person who truly needs him. Such a commitment is good, he argues, and so must be from God.

Here the discernment is much trickier than in the case of the enthusiastic movements. The "end" is not clearly evil; in fact it is a great good, one of the principal reasons for the sacramentality of marriage. But is it good *for this priest*, who has made a stable commitment to One already, and who has been effective in the ministry consequent upon that commitment? Is the change a sign of the tail of the snake precisely because it leads to a lesser good for the church and for this man? Just ask yourself: If you were the devil, how would you work to destroy the commitment of a pious and effective priest?[4]

Of course, not all the evil spirit's deceits have such dramatic or far-reaching effects. At times, as St. Ignatius says, his false consolations "may end in what weakens the soul, or disquiets it or . . . causes disturbance to the soul." For example, he may inspire fervor and devotion in a retreat in order to generate unrealistic expectations for the future, to lead us to promise the Lord something that is beyond our strength. If I make promises at a time of devotion which I cannot keep in the cold light of day, the end result will be discouragement and a failure to do even the good which is possible. If I resolve never to have sensual thoughts again, which is clearly impossible barring a miracle of grace, I may well end up deciding that the whole struggle to be chaste and faithful in my love is a hopeless enterprise. Similarly, the evil spirit can fill devout souls committed to the apostolate with a strong desire for the contemplative life, only to leave them

---

4 Imagining what you would do if you were the devil is an extremely effective way to unmask him. The classic use of this technique is C.S. Lewis' great *Screwtape Letters* (N.Y. Doubleday Image, 1981), which is the correspondence of a senior devil in hell to his nephew and spiritual directee, who is an apprentice devil on earth.

restless, anxious and dissatisfied with their present state and obligations.

Fortunately, the good spirit is also at work in our lives. Many of our consolations and inspirations to act are truly from him. We can recognize them by their consistent goodness throughout. As St. Ignatius tells us: "If the beginning and middle and end of the course of (our) thoughts are wholly good and directed to what is entirely right, it is a sign that they are from the good angel." Nonetheless, the preceding pages can be a bit discouraging at first sight. One could easily feel that, given the manifold ways the evil spirit can sow weeds in the field of the Lord, there is very little hope for the average soul to journey safely through what appears to be a minefield. But this is not so. It is true that things are more complex and tricky than we naively assume; but discernment is an art: What appears complex at first blush becomes much easier with experience. The important thing, as St. Ignatius tells us in the one rule which we have not yet considered, is that we learn from our experience. The devil can be a treacherous adversary; but in the end the poor fellow, quite against his will, also proves to be one of our best teachers, a real instrument of our sanctification!

Practicum Question

Would the consolations of the blind man and of Zacchaeus (Lk 18:35-19:10) be with or without cause? Do you see any sign of the tail of the snake in either incident? What about the people in John 6:1-15 (cf. 25-27)? And Peter in John 6:67-71?

Chapter 8
The Value of Weeds

Of all the evangelists, only Matthew recounts the parable of the weeds and the wheat. It forms part of the discourse in parables, which in turn is found in the fourth of seven sections of his gospel, "The Mystery of the Kingdom of Heaven."[1] After the proclamation of the kingdom by Jesus in the Sermon on the Mount and its initial preaching by missionaries sent out by Jesus himself, this central section treats of "the obstacles with which the kingdom will meet from men, and which are part of God's deliberate design that the kingdom should come without show, even imperceptibly, as illustrated in the parables of the concluding instruction."[2]

A Mysterious Kingdom

The kingdom, then, is mysterious. It is unlike the kingdoms of this world and comes in a way contrary to human expectations, and it elicits a mysterious response from those who do perceive its coming. Jesus employs seven parables (in St. Matthew's account) to explain the mystery of his kingdom to his hearers: the sower, the weeds and the wheat, the mustard seed, the yeast, the "treasure hidden in a field," the pearl of great price, and the "dragnet cast into the sea." Of the seven, which reveal diverse aspects of the mystery of the kingdom, none perhaps is more

---

1 See *The Jerusalem Bible* (Doubleday, 1966), p. 12 of *The New Testament* section, for the accepted contemporary division of Matthew's gospel into seven sections (seven being the Jewish symbol of perfection or completeness), comprising "a dramatic account in seven acts of the coming of the kingdom of heaven." Each of the sections, except the first (the infancy narrative as a prologue to or preparation for the kingdom's coming) and the last (the fulfillment of the kingdom in the paschal mystery), consists of a narrative section and then a discourse by Jesus drawing out the meaning of the narrated events.

2 *Loc. cit.*

mysterious than the story of the weeds and the wheat. This is the way Matthew recounts it:

> He put another parable before them. "The kingdom of heaven may be compared to a man who sowed good seed in his field. While everybody was asleep his enemy came, sowed weeds all among the wheat, and made off. When the new wheat sprouted and ripened, the weeds appeared as well. The owner's servants went to him and said, 'Sir, was it not good seed that you sowed in your field? If so, where do the weeds come from?' 'Some enemy has done this,' he answered. And the servants said, 'Do you want us to go and weed it out?' But he said, 'No, because when you pull out the weeds you might pull up the wheat with them. Let them both grow till the harvest; and at harvest time I shall say to the reapers: First collect the weeds and tie them into bundles to be burnt, then gather the wheat into my barn' " (Mt 13:24-30).

In St. Matthew's account, only two of the parables are explained by Jesus: the sower and this one concerning the weeds and the wheat. Of the latter he says:

> "The sower of the good seed is the Son of Man (the Messiah). The field is the world, the good seed is the subjects of the kingdom; the weeds, the subjects of the evil one; the enemy who sowed them, the devil; the harvest is the end of the world; the reapers are the angels" (Mt 13:38-39).

In its primary meaning, then, the parable is presented as referring to the coexistence in this life of good and evil men and women, of those "planted" by Jesus himself and those planted by the devil. Why does God allow evil men to exist and to corrupt the field which is this world of ours? By any normal human standard, this "fifth column" of the devil should be rooted out if the kingdom is to prosper and come to full fruition. Yet, the parable tells us, it is not so in the mystery of the kingdom of heaven. Here the weeds must be allowed to coexist with the wheat until the harvest, lest in uprooting the weeds "you might pull up the wheat with them." Apparently the weeds and the wheat are so entangled in the field of this world that one could not be uprooted without endangering the other.

This primary meaning of the parable would indicate that the lives of good and of evil men and women are entwined in the world's field, that they draw life from the same soil and even are in some sort of symbiotic (mutually sustaining) relationship to each other. This is indeed true (though paradoxical),[3] but I believe we can extend the parable even further without doing violence to the meaning intended by Jesus himself. That is, as St. Paul indicates in Romans 7 in discussing the two "laws" at work within himself, we may also take the "field" to be the soul of the individual believer. Here too both good and evil seed is sown, the former by the Son of Man and the latter by the evil one. Both weeds and wheat sprout and grow in this personal field; and the mysterious fact is that it seems we must allow the weeds to grow until the harvest, lest "when you pull out the weeds you might pull up the wheat with them."

When we understand the parable in this way, as referring to the field which is the soul of the Christian, we can see that some at least of our instinctual and involuntary weaknesses are likely to remain in us until the harvest time of death. The Lord leaves them in us to keep us humble, to make us realize how totally we depend on him and how helpless we are to do good without his grace and his power. The wheat of our virtues—trust, humility, gratitude, zeal—could not come to full maturity, it seems, without the weeds of our instinctual failings.[4] This, clearly, is the lesson St. Paul learned from the Lord when he begged that the "sting of the flesh" be removed from his life and was told by him: "My grace is enough for you: my power is at its best in weakness." That this did not mean the Lord's grace would remove Paul's "sting" here and now is clear from the conclusion he draws:

> So I shall be very happy to make my weaknesses my special boast so that the power of Christ may stay over me, and that is why I am quite content with my weaknesses, and with insults, hardships, persecutions, and the agonies I go through for Christ's sake. For it is when I am weak that I am strong (2 Cor 12:9-10).

Paul had to live with his weaknesses—and with the "agonies"

---

3 See our discussion in *Darkness in the Marketplace, Chapter 5.*

4 Cf. chapter 2 of *When the Well Runs Dry.*

(desolations) that resulted from them—until the harvest time when the weeds, having served their purpose in him, could be definitively uprooted.

How many of us really understand, in our own lives, the lesson Paul learned here? It seems to me it is a rare soul who can truly glory in her infirmity, and exercise the patience of God with respect to the involuntary weaknesses of others as well as her own. Even when we do realize "in the head" that these weaknesses are really for our growth in humility and trust, we still hope "in the heart" that they will be gone when we awake tomorrow! That, at least, is my own experience. And I would not be surprised to learn St. Paul *felt* the same way much of the time, despite his beautiful words of acceptance.

The Educative Value of Weeds

For this reason, I (and all who find their reactions are not so different from mine) need to return often to Jesus' parable of the weeds and the wheat. We need to be reminded often of the mysterious intertwining of weeds and wheat in the harvest field of the kingdom of God within us. And we need to probe deeper to discover the meaning and purpose of this mystery. Unless we do so—unless we can accept the weeds in the faith-spirit of St. Paul and learn the lesson of our infirmity—these weeds *could* choke the wheat and destroy the harvest. It is not enough to let them survive; they must survive for a purpose, serve a good end. This means that we must see them with eyes of discerning love, of discernment. When we do so, they become the instrument of our deepening trust and humility. They purify us. They make us true floaters in the sea of the Lord.

This purifying, cross-fertilizing value of the weeds in our lives is not, however, their only value. There is also what we might call the educative value of these weeds in our interior lives. It is to this educative value that St. Ignatius refers in the sixth of the second week rules for discernment, the only rule we have not yet considered. He says there:

> When the enemy of our human nature has been detected and recognized by the trail of evil marking his course and by the wicked end to which he leads us, it will be profit-

able for one who has been tempted to review immediately the whole course of the temptation. Let him consider the series of good thoughts, how they arose, how the evil one gradually attempted to make him step down from the state of spiritual delight and joy in which he was, till finally he drew him to his wicked designs. The purpose of this review is that once such an experience has been understood and carefully observed, we may guard ourselves for the future against the customary deceits of the enemy (#336).

The principle enunciated here by St. Ignatius is one which is applicable even outside the spiritual domain. We recall Socrates' famous dictum that "the unexamined life is not worth living." And it was Santayana, I believe, who said that those who ignore the past are condemned to repeat its mistakes. We all make mistakes; but it is the mark of the wise man or woman to learn from his or her errors. If we do learn from them, then they are not disasters but rather an essential part of our growth. As I often find myself telling the seminarians when they approach ordination, "You will surely make many mistakes in the course of your life and ministry. But be sure they are *new* mistakes! Don't keep making the same ones over and over again." If we do continually repeat the same errors, it means we have learned nothing from our experience.

In the area of discernment, this means that we must be prepared to examine and evaluate our religious experiences, to review the whole course of such an experience, in order to determine which spirits were at work and what tactics they employed. Many of these tactics have been uncovered by St. Ignatius in the rules we have discussed. Since, however, the evil spirit is like a shrewd military tactician who studies his target (ourselves) and probes for areas of vulnerability, we also have to discover which of these tactics he finds most effective in attacking us. In the process, of course, we learn a great deal about ourselves, our own strengths and weaknesses.

Many people find this kind of self-analysis too "introspective." They feel it would destroy spontaneity and thus they would prefer just to live naturally—to love, to pray, to serve—without continually looking over their shoulders and observing themselves. This is a valid objection, in the sense that we must strike a proper balance between spontaneity and reflective evaluation. It is *not* good to be continually censoring ourselves: If we analyze every step we take as we are taking it, we will never get anywhere, and we may well stumble over our own feet. Sometimes I sense this with good people who come for direction and cannot complete a single sentence without correcting and editing themselves five or ten times. They become entangled in their own self-censorship (a form of scrupulosity, perhaps) with the result that it becomes very difficult, for them as well as for me, to discover what they are really experiencing. On the other hand, there are many people who never examine their experiences and as a result are condemned to a continual repetition of the same disappointments and frustrations. Their life is like a treadmill, with continual motion but no progress.

How do we strike the proper balance? In the first place, we must know ourselves: Do I tend to be overanalytical, or too uncritical and naive? Here, too, the evil spirit is a shrewd tactician. If I am an anxious, perfectionist type, he will encourage this excessive analysis and call it virtue. If, on the other hand, I tend to be shallow and unreflective, he will seek to reinforce my weakness by calling it spontaneity and naturalness. In both cases he will try to make a virtue out of a vice in order to prevent us from growing and maturing. In order to combat him effectively, it is essential that we have a solid, realistic knowledge of our own temperament.

Another practical guideline in balancing experience and reflective evaluation is to realize that there is a time and a season for each. In the *Spiritual Exercises*, St. Ignatius tells the retreatant to spend some time after the prayer is finished reflecting on how it went and what happened. Today we normally do this by means of the prayer journal. But note we do this after, not during, the prayer. In fact, I always tell retreatants that one great value of the journal is to prevent ourselves from looking over our shoulders and analyzing our experience during the prayer. It is not good to be continually turning away from God to analyze what is happening. That would destroy any human encounter. Even if we are "on the wrong track," we cannot go far wrong in just one hour of prayer. Thus it is much better, I believe, to wait until we finish the prayer to evaluate what really happened.[5] And the same principle applies to our daily prayer and faith life outside of retreat. This is why the consciousness examen — a prayerful review of the ways God has been speaking, and how I have responded, in the day just past — is such a valuable part of any genuine Christian spirituality. It fosters a habitual and on-the-spot sensitivity to the ways the various spirits work in all the events of our lives.

Encounter and Afterglow

In chapter 7 we saw the distinction drawn by St. Ignatius between consolation with a preceding cause and without such a cause. As we explained it, the cause in question would be some sensible experience or reflection — a beautiful sunrise, meditation on a scripture passage, praise from a friend or superior, etc. — which occasioned an experience of religious consolation. When consolation is experienced without any such cause, we can be sure, St. Ignatius tells us, that the experience is from God himself. The danger here, as we explained, is that we may confuse the actual time of genuine consolation with the afterglow, when the soul is still in a state of consolation but is no longer in direct contact with the Lord. "At such a time the soul is still fervent and favored with the grace and aftereffects of the consolation which has passed. In this second period the soul frequently forms various resolutions and plans which are not granted directly by God our Lord" (rule 8, #336).

This is one instance where it can be most helpful to follow Ignatius' advice to review the whole experience later and discover how the evil spirit insinuated himself. An example from my own experience might help to make this clear. Some years ago in the Philippines, a seminarian from one of the nearby seminaries came to visit me at the end of summer vacation. He had recently completed the equivalent of what we at San Jose call the Spiritual-

---

5 As we shall see in chapter 9, there will be a certain spontaneous, "instinctive" discernment as we pray, particularly as we mature and become more sensitive to the normal workings of the good and evil spirits in our lives. But this is unselfconscious and spontaneous; it does not interrupt the natural flow of our experience.

Pastoral Formation Year—a sort of novitiate year for diocesan seminarians after second-year theology—toward the end of which he had made a 30-day retreat. Shortly after the retreat he and the others had returned to their own dioceses for vacation. Now, when he came into my room, he appeared quite dejected. I greeted him and then asked what was disturbing him. He said, "I feel I am a failure. The 30-day retreat, only three months ago, was a beautiful experience and I felt I really encountered the Lord and was confirmed in my vocation. And yet it seems that during the summer I have broken *every* promise I then made to him." He was disappointed and ashamed, and I am sure it seemed to him the whole retreat was fruitless.

My heart went out to him. But what to say? By the grace of God, the right words came to my lips: "Can you recall the situation in retreat when you made those promises to the Lord? Did the inspiration come from you or from him? That is, are you sure that what you promised was really what *he* was asking?" I went on to explain why I asked the question, and as I finished he said: "As soon as you asked, I knew the promises had come from *me*. I can recall the time when I was deciding what to promise the Lord in return for his love, and I had a very strong sense he was saying to me, 'Are you sure you can really do all this?' It was as if he was doubtful, but in my enthusiasm I assured him I could!"

The "evil spirit" had insinuated himself into the scene. Most likely my seminarian-friend had truly been encountering the Lord,[6] but in the afterglow of his consolation he had been inspired—and *not* by the Lord!—to make promises which were beyond his present strength. As he and I now reflected on the experience together, we could both learn valuable lessons for the future. He could, and presumably did, learn to be more cautious in committing himself to projects and plans which might appear easy on the mountaintop in the afterglow of the Lord's passing, but which were unrealistic in the valley when the morning fog covered the sun. And I learned the danger of urging retreatants to commit themselves to a plan of life, as is often done in retreats.

---

6 Whether this encounter was with or without cause is not really essential to our point here. It could have been either one.

Such a plan is good and valuable, but only if it is brought to the Lord for his confirmation and ratification. What he desires we can surely accomplish. But we have to be sure he really desires it! His grace must be behind our efforts; otherwise the failure to accomplish our goals can easily lead to discouragement and the abandonment of our whole commitment to the Lord. This, of course, is precisely what the evil spirit desires, and he is willing to sing Gregorian chant to accomplish it.

A Heightened Sensitivity

Thus, if we are faithful to the consciousness examen, and to the advice of St. Ignatius to review our experiences in order that "we may guard ourselves for the future against the customary deceits of the enemy," we will soon learn to distinguish between the genuine experience of God and its dangerous "afterglow." Moreover, we will become much more sensitive to the diverse ways in which both God and the evil spirit work in us. This sensitivity is at the very heart of the art of spiritual direction, in two senses. The good director is one who has a keen, experientially grounded sensitivity to the various species of weeds and of wheat which are usually found in the harvest field of the soul. Secondly, the primary purpose of direction is to bring the directee to this same sensitivity. As we stressed in chapter 3, good direction fosters not dependency but mature responsibility. The successful director, like the successful teacher, produces souls who can stand on their own, who can read the signs of the times, and of the diverse spirits at work in their own lives.

On the positive side, this means discovering what our God is like and how he works in our lives. Jesus, of course, is *the* revelation of the Father for us. The gospels, above all, teach us what kind of person the God and Father of Jesus Christ is. But the history of Christianity makes clear how variously this revelation can be interpreted, and how narrow and suffocating a blindly fundamentalist or legalistic interpretation can be. The gospels truly come alive only for those who are led by them to a *personal* experience of the God who is the Father of Jesus. That is why the meditative prayer of beginners is a continual interplay and interpenetration of personal experience and the scriptural revelation.[7] Each sheds light on the other, and in the mutual interplay we come to know the Lord at work in our own lives.

What does this mean concretely? I suppose the facets of the mystery of God which we may discover in our personal experience are truly infinite in number. But certain basic discoveries seem to characterize every good prayer life. For example, that our God works very slowly: He is infinitely patient with us, and we must be just as patient with him and with ourselves. In this respect the parable of the weeds and the wheat really seems to describe the way he handles his planting. Also, he seems to be much more receptive to gratitude than to complaints. At least, if my own experience is any gauge, thankfulness and trust are by far the best ways to "blackmail" him and to reach his heart. And I gather he does like to be blackmailed in this way, just as he likes those who can approach him naturally and spontaneously, who can be "naked" and without masks before him. All of this, and whatever else we may discover of the Lord in a life of discerning love, is really but the gospel portrait which Jesus draws of his Father. Yet how many, even among those who can quote the scriptures at length, seem to have a very different picture of God!

Different Species of Weeds

Why is it that scripture can be so difficult to interpret and can lead different people to such mutually conflicting and even contradictory images of God? Could it be that we hear what we want or expect to hear, and that we are limited in our openness to the whole of Jesus' revelation of his father by our own biases and fears? I think so. Yet this is but to say that many weeds grow up along with the wheat of faith in our hearts. This is true even in the most generous of pray-ers and apostles. In some, the weeds of timidity and scrupulosity prevent them from experiencing the gentleness and patience of the Good Shepherd. For others, the weeds of self-reliance and energetic activism make dependence on the "Holy God! Strong God! Immortal God!" of the Good Friday liturgy equally difficult to accept and experience. Whatever the weeds may be in our own particular wheat field, they bid fair to

---

7 See chapter 6 of *Opening to God*.

choke off the wheat of faith and good works which the Lord has planted.

There is hope, however, even though many of these weeds seem destined to survive until the harvest. For those who are faithful to prayer and seek to grow in discerning love, the experiential knowledge of which we spoke earlier is not only a knowledge of God. We also come to know the various species of weeds which we called in chapter 3 "the world, the flesh and the devil." We cannot completely eliminate many of them from our lives until the day we die, but the more we know about them by experience the less danger there is that they will destroy the harvest, at least if our knowledge is put at the service of our love. In fact, they can positively contribute to the growth and maturing of the wheat, just as Satan (contrary to his own intentions!) did in leading Job to great holiness, and as many parasites and pests do in the world of nature.

What do we need to know of these weeds in order that they serve our ends and not we theirs? What do we learn of the three species — world, flesh, and devil — from the scriptures[8] and from our own experience as discerned in the light of scripture? It seems to me, first of all, that the "world" can be taken to mean the whole complex of values and attitudes — the culture — which we absorb with our mother's milk. This milieu may be more or less Christian, but it is never wholly and authentically Christian in the gospel sense. In a footnote to chapter 1 of St. John's gospel (1g), *The Jerusalem Bible* points out that the "world" in St. John has various meanings: "the cosmos or this earth, the human race, those hostile to God who hate Christ and his disciples," with an enumeration of several passages in which John uses "world" in this latter, pejorative sense. St. Paul sometimes uses the word in this sense (e.g., Gal 1:4, "this present wicked world"); and he also uses it to refer to the material world, not as specifically evil but as in need of redemption (Rom 8:19-22, cf. *The Jerusalem Bible* footnote k). Thus the Christian can never have a simplistically

---

8 For a very good summary of the scriptural doctrine, see the "Index of Biblical Themes" in *The Jerusalem Bible*, pp. 498 ("world"), 487 ("flesh") and 485 ("devil"). The references (e.g., John 1g) are to the fine footnotes (John, chapter 1, footnote g) to the text. See also John McKenzie, *Dictionary of the Bible*.

romantic view of this world. It is not simply evil, but neither is it unqualifiedly good—at least not until the redemptive power of Jesus Christ, for which it "groans" (Rom 8:22), has transformed it.

The values of this world, taken as sinful and unredeemed, are enumerated in 1 John 2:16 as follows: "The sensual body, the lustful eye, pride in possession." At times the values may not be so pernicious, and yet neither are they wholly Christic. The point is that this is the air we breathe—our culture, our family nurture. What is wrong with abortion? Or with couples living together, without benefit of marriage, as long as they truly love one another? Shouldn't I look out for "number one," myself, above all; after all, if you don't love yourself, who will? All of these, and many more like them, are questions which our "world" today puts to us. Those of us who grew up in another world, with another set of values, may see the obvious fallacy in many of the challenges of the world today. But what of those who never knew another world? After all, we "old-timers" lived comfortably with racial discrimination and inequitable social structures which would be abhorrent today. The trouble with the weeds of the world is that often we don't recognize them as weeds.

I sometimes wonder if this is not a significant part of the mystery of Jimmy Carter's presidency. It seems to be a truism today to say that he was a committed Christian and a man of high moral principle, but a poor politician who did not understand the uses of power. But what do we mean by a "good politician"? And what is the paradigm of a proper use of power? Can one be a committed and uncompromising follower of Jesus Christ and, at the same time, a successful wielder of political power? We surely want to say that it is possible. Yet, while the United States (like other countries) has had several presidents who were men of principles and ideals, there are few who have revealed that the will of God and the following of Christ were central concerns in their decisions and actions.

Jimmy Carter did claim this. We would like to say, perhaps, that the failure to integrate discerning love into political leadership was a personal failure, or limitation, on his part—that the right man (or woman), with both political genius and genuine religious commitment, could successfully integrate the two. But I wonder. Perhaps Abraham Lincoln is the American president who, despite his lack of formal religious affiliation, seemed to succeed best in being a man of God and a successful political leader. Yet, was Lincoln really "successful" in the eyes of his contemporaries? He did win re-election, but he did so in the middle of a major war effort when incumbent leaders are rarely set aside. Lincoln himself seems to have felt keenly the frustrations and failures of his presidency; inspired political leadership and high moral principle were not at all easy to reconcile in his time either. The fact that we "canonize" him today may be but a further proof that it is easier to venerate a dead and distant man of religious conviction than it is to accept him in life. Even Jesus himself is much easier for us to accept and venerate today because the world of the Pharisees—the worldly values which he denounced in his own culture—is not really our world. We might react very differently if he were to confront us directly, and challenge our accepted secular values today.

This is really the point we were exploring: What is this "world" which militates against the work of the Spirit of God in our lives? It is the cultural air we breathe, the whole complex of values and attitudes which are not really godly, but which we take for granted until the voice of the good spirit breaks into our lives and forces us to question them. Such values are among the weeds that will remain until the harvest. Some of them can be rooted out of us, in which case, while they do not block our own discernment, they survive in the "unconverted" milieu in which we live our lives. They, or the people who hold them, are a continual challenge to and purifying force for our commitment to the Lord.

Unfortunately, however, things are not all as simple as that. This worldly milieu is not simply something outside of us. Nor is the conflict between good and evil a black-and-white, "good guys and bad guys" conflict like the classic cowboy and Indian movies. The "world" of unredeemed and un-Christlike values survives to some degree even *within* the best of us. Some of the weeds of the world do seem to cling to life even in the soil most receptive to God's planting. Why is this so? It is, it seems to me, because the second of the biblical weeds — the "flesh" — already is deeply rooted there. St. John of the Cross says that only the dark night of the soul, the deepest and ultimate purification of souls totally given to God, can completely eradicate the roots of sin in us. Even the passive night of senses merely cuts off the weeds at ground level; it does not get to the roots. St. Paul, I believe, is referring to the same experience in Romans 7, where he speaks of the two laws that he, and every person, finds in himself: the law which is "spiritual" and the law of sin, of the flesh, the law "in my members" (7:23).

This latter law is the "inordinate attachments" which the *Spiritual Exercises* of St. Ignatius (see #1 in the text) are directed to freeing us from. It is the "desires" of St. John of the Cross' *Dark Night* and *Ascent of Mount Carmel*, those desires which war against our transformation in God and which only he can completely remove from our lives. This biblical "flesh" is the lower element in every man and woman which is distinguished from "spirit" (*pneuma*) and often opposed to it. Flesh can mean merely the bodily element in human beings, but often, and especially, it refers to the sphere in which sin and passions operate in us.[9] In this latter sense, the flesh is gradually purified and transformed by the work of God in us.

Again, however, we never achieve full freedom from our inner vanity and sensuality in this life. Even the best and most generous of souls have to live with the vestigial weeds of disordered self-love, the ultimate root of all the various species of weeds which appear in the wheat field. There are, for example, those involuntary faults which persist in us even when the water of prayer is flowing abundantly.[10] Their presence is not a sign that our prayer life is insincere or fruitless. It is true that our spiritual life would be suspect if there were no growth at all in these areas of instinctual, involuntary weakness. But what growth there is may be frustratingly slow, precisely because the Lord knows we *need* these weeds to teach us true humility. As we

9 See *The Jerusalem Bible*, footnotes 1g and 7d to "Romans" for a good summary of the meanings of "flesh" in Paul and of the passages where the word is used in a "sinful" sense.

10 We discussed this in chapter 2 of *When the Well Runs Dry*.

said earlier in this present chapter, if we could completely master these failings we might easily forget how totally we depend on God and his grace. Thus the instinctual weeds, the flesh in us, play an important role in the growth of the good wheat of humility and trust. And the flesh in others—their envy and mistrust of us, for example—also play an important role in our sanctification: Because of those obstacles, we learn that ultimately we can find full acceptance and complete understanding only in the good Lord himself. No human being can know us totally and affirm us in the very depths of our being.

Thus we see that the weeds of the flesh, like the weeds of the world, do have a value in our lives. What of the third species of weeds, the "devil"? In the scripture he is the cause of the troubles of world and flesh, the ultimate evil genius behind the planting and cultivating of these weeds in our harvest field. As Paul says toward the end of Ephesians:

> Put God's armor on so as to be able to resist the devil's tactics. For it is not against human enemies that we have to struggle but against the Sovereignties and Powers who originate the darkness in this world, the spiritual army of evil in the heavens (6:11-12).

And in 2 Corinthians 4:4, Paul calls the evil spirit "the god of this world," who blinds unbelievers to the true light of Christ's gospel. Later in the same letter (12:7), Paul's famous thorn in the flesh is identified as "an angel of Satan."

Clearly the evils of the world and the flesh are closely connected in the New Testament revelation with the work of the devil in our lives. In addition, however, the devil is seen as the cause of demonic possession (Mt 8:29 and ff.; 12:43-45) as seeking to divulge the messianic secret of Jesus before the proper time (Mk 1:34). He inspires Judas to betray Jesus (Jn 13:2), and he even mimics Christ and the Spirit in working miracles to seduce believers (Rv 13:15).[11] In short, he is the "father of lies" of whom

---

11 See McKenzie, *Dictionary of the Bible*, under "demon" and "Satan," as well as *The Jerusalem Bible*, footnotes Matthew 8j, Mark 1i, John 13e, 1 Peter 5h, and Revelation 13g, for a full discussion of the New Testament understanding of Satan's role in Christian life.

Jesus speaks in John 8:44. He can work not only through the natural means of the world and the flesh but also directly on the mind and heart of man, although only, as St. John of the Cross tells us, through the senses. This is why consolation with sensible cause, as we have seen in chapter 7, cannot be uncritically accepted as coming from God. Miracles, visions, the secrets of God, all can be used by the evil spirit to accomplish his own ends.

The thought that the devil can seduce even the pious by "pious" means is a disturbing one. Yet even his seductions work to good for those who truly love God. This, perhaps, is the most striking point about the great Book of Job. As we have said, Satan's efforts to destroy Job result, in the end, in Job's sanctification. The dark night through which he passes purifies his love and deepens his trust. At the end of the trial, when Yahweh returns and sheds his light on Job's searing experience, he can say in reply: "I have been holding forth on matters I cannot understand, on marvels beyond me and my knowledge. . . . I knew you then by hearsay; but now, having seen you with my own eyes, I retract all I have said" (42:3,5).

Conclusion

Thus even the weed which we call the devil has a value in the wheat field of the Lord. Quite contrary to his own intentions, he — like the world and the flesh who are his minions — can become the sandpaper of the sanctification of God's beloved ones. For them, who are called according to God's purpose, "everything works for good." So it is that "neither death nor life, no angel, no prince, nothing that exists, nothing still to come, . . . nor any created thing, can ever come between us and the love of God made visible in Christ Jesus our Lord" (Rom 8:28, 38-39). This working for good is not automatic, of course. The world and the flesh and the devil have other, quite contrary ends in view. The weeds can choke the wheat and destroy the good harvest. But for those whose lives are lived in discerning love, who are alert and sensitive to the dangers and values of these weeds, their very presence and challenge assure a more abundant harvest.

Practicum Question

We said early in this chapter that the devil, like a shrewd military tactician, probes our defenses and attacks where he finds us weakest. Which of the various weeds which we have discussed — world, flesh, and devil — do you think he would find most effective in the world of today? Which would be most effective in his attacks on you personally?

Chapter 9
The Wheat Matures: Discerning Love

Not long ago, I had occasion to meet a charming lady with whom I had been corresponding for several months. Her name is Joan Sherry, and she lives on the Isle of Wight — the only person I have ever known from that enchanted outpost of England! When she first wrote to me in the Philippines, she explained her writing in this way: "During the early part of October I spent a lovely week in Rome, staying with my godchild, who is a Salvatorian sister at their international motherhouse there. On the morning of my departure I made a last visit to St. Peter's, and then to the Ancora bookshop nearby, for some last-minute purchases from their print and art department. The Ancora bookstore in Rome is a fairly big establishment, and when my footsteps led me to the 'English' section, I wondered why I went right around the central stand, ignoring the shelf displays around the walls, lifted up two larger volumes, picked up a copy of *When the Well Runs Dry*, and took it straight over to the desk to purchase. When I got home to England I began to read it (after my morning prayers), and seeing 'March 19, 1979, Feast of San Jose' after the preface, made me think that somebody certainly nudged my elbow in that shop!"

March 19, 1979, happened to be the day I had written and dated the preface to the *Well*. St. Joseph has played an important role in my life, from my birth on his feast to my education with the Sisters of St. Joseph, and my assignment for the past 14 years — the longest I have ever lived in one place — at San Jose Seminary in Manila. Even more, I have found in Joseph a true father and friend; he seems to embody everything in a man that I would like to be. I think I understand why Jesus, having known Joseph as his human father, would find "Father" the perfect

161

name for the God he came to reveal to us.

For Joan Sherry, the significance of my reference to March 19, 1979, is expressed in the following lines from that first letter she wrote to me: "Peter and I were married on March 19, 1951, and of course we always regarded St. Joseph as the patron and protector of our marriage and home. Something very special happened to me on the night of the 19th of March, 1979, and it was the reason for me writing the enclosed small book. I do hope you may like to read it." I did read the "enclosed small book" and found it to be delightful, well-written and truly moving. It is called *Dance for Your Uncle Sam*, the reference being not to the United States but to a saying of Peter Sherry's father, when he was coaching the two youngest of his five sons and four daughters (all of whom followed him into the "theatre" or vaudeville) to dance and do acrobatics. When Peter and Sam were being pressed to perform for relatives and friends, their father, Dan, would say, "If you dance for your Uncle Sam, perhaps he'll give you a thousand pounds!"[1]

Uncle Sam never came up with the thousand pounds, but Peter Sherry did go on to a life in the English theatre, a meeting with the young singer-comedienne, Joan, in 1947, and marriage to her on March 19, 1951. They had the misfortune to come on the scene just as the "theatre" was succumbing to television, and so in 1956 they retired to the Isle of Wight to run a guest house and "caravan" park. Here they lived a happy, almost idyllic life until, in 1967, Peter suffered a cerebral thrombosis which left him a semi-invalid. The years that followed were difficult, purifying ones for both of them, a true marketplace darkness that, by the grace of God, strengthened and deepened their love for him and for each other. In 1979, while they were on vacation in the Canary Islands, Peter died suddenly of a pulmonary embolism. The date was March 5, shortly before the dedication date of the *Well* which led Joan Sherry to write to me.

---

1 Joan Sherry, *Dance for Your Uncle Sam*, p. 4. The book is privately printed (1981), and may be obtained from Conroy Books, 4 Wilkes Road, Sandown, Isle of Wight, PO36 8EZ, England.

Experience, Afterglow and the Habit of Discerning Love

With all the formalities attendant upon transferring a body from one country to another, it was not until March 15 that Peter Sherry was buried on the Isle of Wight. Three days later, on the eve of their 28th wedding anniversary and of the feast of St. Joseph, Joan says (p. 72), "I went to bed as usual, and although of course I was feeling very sad, and the tears came often, as they do to everyone at first, I was not sleeping badly. . . . I am not a person who has dreams, I dream very seldom, and usually only after a heavy dinner too late in the evening." On this night, however, she had a very unusual experience: "I cannot even consider referring to it as a dream, because I know that it was quite different in every characteristic from any dream that I had ever had. Every detail of it is sharp and clear in my mind."

It was this unusual experience, in the early morning hours of March 19, 1979, which led Joan to write *Dance for Your Uncle Sam* — and to write to me. It also led, in the end, to our meeting in Dublin, as a result of which I asked her permission to refer to the incident in this book. It brings out clearly and beautifully, I believe, much of what we have discussed about the discernment of consolation; and, in addition, it helps to situate such experiences in the context of a total life, a habitual pattern of discerning love.

First, this is how Joan describes the experience (p. 73):

I was looking toward a group of very large trees — I could not say what sort of trees they were because I couldn't see the tops of them or their leaves — but I was looking through the groups of trees with their big trunks, smooth almost like beech trees, and on the far side could see a broad, green meadow. There was a crowd of people, all moving in the same direction, from left to right, on the far side of the trees, until they passed from my sight. After a while the crowd thinned, until they were in small groups, then three's and two's — and then last of all, by himself, was Peter.

At first I felt a tremendous and overwhelming sense of excitement, which I appreciate must have been expected in the circumstances. Seeing him again would of course have aroused the strongest feelings in me. But I can only say that it was an excitement that I find myself unable to compare with anything at all that I had experienced in my whole life.

I was propelled forcibly forward, by what I can best describe as a tremendous surge of electric energy, calling his name loudly, and saying, "Where are you?" As I reached him, he turned and faced me directly, looking straight into my eyes, putting out his hands, and taking both of my hands in both of his.

I could not say if it was Peter as he was just before he died, or whether as a younger man, neither could I recall what he was wearing, although I tried very hard to do so afterwards. In other words, I think the recognition was not the sort that we have of each other here and now. I recognized, as it were, the whole of his personality, the entire Being, not little details of it.

And when I asked him where he was, he looked at me seriously, and said just five words: "I am in the Light." Then it was all gone.

This is the experience which set the final seal on Joan Sherry's love for her Peter and which, in a sense, changed the direction of her life. That it was truly consolation is clear from what she says next: "When I awoke next morning the experience filled my whole mind, and I was very much affected by what had happened to me — a mixture of joy, astonishment, and thankfulness — because I realized at once that the blessing I had been given was a very great one." At the Mass for Peter the next day, March 19, the consolation lingered and at Communion time she "felt the closest possible sharing in the sacrifice that was being offered for us all." Her faith, hope and love were clearly deepened by the experience; specifically, her deepest sense appears to have been of gratitude to the Lord who deigned to lift the veil of death just enough to assure her that her beloved Peter was "in the Light."

Was Joan's consolation with or without preceding sensible cause? Surprisingly, perhaps, I find it difficult to say with certainty. It would seem that her "dream" was a preceding cause in the senses. Yet the details she gives, particularly in the fourth paragraph above about recognizing "the whole of his personality, the entire Being, not little details of it," suggest that this was quite different from our ordinary sense, or dream, experience. Despite this uncertainty, however, I would have little doubt that the experience was a genuine consolation from God. Whether with or without cause, the immediate fruits of the experience all seem to be good, solid signs that it was truly the good spirit at work.

Like many of the significant religious experiences in our lives, though, this one of Joan Sherry's was to have long-range, and not merely immediate, fruits. The experience itself is apparently not as unique as I at first believed: At least two other women have since told me, after they read *Dance for Your Uncle Sam*, of similar dreams after the death of a beloved spouse. What is unique in Joan's case is her later sense that she must share this experience with others, and her writer's gift which enabled her to do so with such moving eloquence. The inspiration to write, though, did not come at the time of the "dream," or even during the consoling hours of the next day. Rather was it the fruit of much reflection on the meaning of her experience and the reasons the Lord might have had for granting it to her. As she says, "It is of course only in retrospect that one sees the overall pattern of events, and I found myself giving a great deal of thought to the significance they might hold" (p. 75). As she reflected on this significance, it seemed to her that this experience of God's love, of confident hope in bereavement, could not be merely for herself alone, that it must be the Lord's intention that she write about it and thus provide hope and strength to others similarly bereaved. This was her answer to the palmist's question, echoing in her own life: "What return can I make to Yahweh for all his goodness to me?" (Ps 116:12).

The point I wanted to make is that Joan Sherry's inspiration to write was *not* part of the consolation experience itself. It might have been: She might have had a strong sense during her "dream" that the Lord (or Peter) was telling her, "You must write about this so others will be strengthened in their bereavement." But this did not happen to her. In some sense, the inspiration to write her book came during the "afterglow" of her experience when her own faculties and senses were quite active in searching out the meaning of what had happened. This being the case, as we have seen in chapter 7, we cannot automatically assume—even assuming the consolation experience itself was genuine and from the good spirit — that the call to write a book was also from God. This latter inspiration would have to be tested in the ways we have already described: by examining the "beginning, middle and end" of the experience to see if all are good, and, as Joan Sherry seems to have done, by bringing back to the Lord in prayer the idea of sharing her experience in writing. The test of consolation and peace, when she did so — as well as submitting the plan to the judgment of a good director — would provide the necessary confirmation that the projected book was the Lord's will.

There is, however, an even more striking aspect to Joan Sherry's story. We have entitled this section, "Experience, Afterglow, and the Habit of Discerning Love." In Joan's case, we have seen the experience and the afterglow. But what of that "habit of discerning love"? First of all, what do we mean by it? We have seen in chapter 3, in discussing the example of choosing neckties, that growth in a love relationship brings with it a *habitual* sensitivity to what pleases the beloved. Joe and Letty and Ed and Maria, being young and inexperienced, lacked this biblical "knowledge" of the Lord. That is why they needed the help of a "co-discerner" who possessed it. And, as we said there, the fruit of good direction should be a growth in this sensitivity on the part of the directee — not merely a solution to the specific, immediate problem to be discerned, but a "feel" for what pleases the Lord in future discernment situations. This feel, this "instinctive" sensitivity, is one important element in the habit of discerning love.

Joan Sherry, received into the Catholic Church only after her marriage in 1951, traces (unconsciously) the growth of this habit in herself. As is true for most human beings, her growth in instinctive sensitivity to the Lord paralleled, and depended much upon, the growth in her sensitivity to her Peter. Her story makes clear that, through better and worse, she gradually became more and more of one mind and one heart with him. She could read his feelings and true desires, even in those last difficult years when, because of his illness, Peter was not always "his real self." Surely it was not always easy or "intuitive." There were times when it was difficult to know, to understand what was really happening with

Peter; and at such times a sort of "formal discernment," with all the ambiguity that implies, was required of her. But much of the time, because of her long years of loving him, the discernment was habitual, intuitive, "instinctive."

The beautiful thing about Joan Sherry's story is that it reveals a concomitant growth in this habitual sensitivity, this discerning love for the *Lord*. The final pages, where she reflects on the way her dream-experience illuminated her whole past life, make clear that she has journeyed far toward knowing the Lord. The journey, of course, is never finished: Even in eternity, I believe, we shall always be just "beginning" to know him. But she has traveled far from the theater days of 1950 and her first religious instructions from a priest in Glasgow. And it seems quite clear that, for the Joan Sherry of 1981, even her love relationship with Peter is but a means — the most precious means for her — to a life of discerning love with her God.

Our meeting in Dublin confirmed my impression that Joan was a woman at peace with the world, with herself, and with her God. We had never met before but, with the help of an excellent dinner provided by the Cluny sisters, were soon conversing like old friends. We talked about her book and about Peter, discussed what the Lord might have in store for her in the future and, at the end of the afternoon before driving her to the airport to catch a plane back to London, I prevailed upon her to sing for the sisters and me. One song she sang, "If a Picture Paints a Thousand Words, Then Why Can't I Paint You?" plays a special part in her story of Peter's final hours. As she sang it for us, it was easy to see that she was a woman in happy possession of her past. Her life was a unity: sadness and joy, the better and the worse had all fallen into place for her.

This sense of integral peace, it seems to me, is another important aspect of the habit of discerning love of which we spoke. That is, as we come to "know" the Lord in the biblical sense, not only do we develop an intuitive sensitivity to what pleases him in concrete situations. In addition, there is a general at-homeness, a being-at-peace-with the whole flow of our lives. The light and the darkness become essential aspects of a single painting. Our life is not a disconnected jumble of "alarums and excursions," but a unified whole.

I recall being happily surprised, upon meeting and visiting with her, to find the same simple, joyous, peaceful self-possession in Mother Teresa of Calcutta—surprised, because it always struck me as extremely dangerous to canonize someone while they are still alive. Fortunately for her, and almost miraculously, Mother Teresa seemed quite unaware of her overblown press image. I suppose she must be aware of it; perhaps, though, she too has found her Center and is equally aware how unimportant the fickle adulation of the world really is. The habit of discerning love means integration, and integration means simplification. As St. Ignatius says, our only end is the glory of God and our own salvation; everything else on the face of the earth is but a means to this end. Or, in the words of St. Teresa of Avila, "All things pass away. God alone never changes."

Peace and the Feelings

We have described two facets of the habit of discerning love which is the greatest fruit of a life of discernment: an "instinctive" sensitivity to what pleases the Lord in concrete situations; and an integration, a simplification, a centering of our lives on the "one thing necessary." It is important to stress, however, that this does *not* mean that there are no problems, doubts, dark moments. As long as we live by faith and are not confirmed in grace, the evil spirit is always probing and testing and calling into question the centering of our lives. St. Teresa and St. Ignatius, in affirming their centering trust in the Lord, are merely echoing St. Paul when he said that "we know that all things work together unto good for those who love God," that nothing in this world "can ever come between us and the love of God made visible in Christ Jesus our Lord" (Rom 8:28,39). But the context of Paul's triumphant affirmation is his agonized discussion, in Romans 7, of the two "laws" which he finds at war within himself. He sees the good and he truly desires it, and yet, because another "law" is still at work in his flesh, he finds himself, at times, doing what he does not want.

Is Paul "whistling in the dark" in Romans 8? Clearly he is not at peace in the sense that all problems and temptations and doubts are removed from his life. Yet, despite this conflict of the two laws in him, I believe he truly is centered and integrated in the sense we have been discussing. Granted that he is not as integrated and centered as he one day will be, when there is only one law at work in him. But even now, in this "body of death," Paul *wills* only one thing. His instinctual self may not have received the message yet; that is where the other "law" resides in him. Nonetheless, his will's desire is simple: All he truly wants is the love of God. Beyond that, while he must *try* to become integrated if he is truly sincere, ultimately only the grace of God will heal his instinctual self and destroy the other law at work in his members. This, it seems to me, is the whole point of Romans 8 (and of 2 Cor 12:7-10, the "thorn in the flesh"): The victory is the Lord's, and Paul's confidence is grounded not on a realized integration in himself but on a centering hope that the Lord surely will bring to perfection the good work that *he* has begun. Meanwhile, Paul possesses a mysterious and paradoxical peace, the sign that he lives in "the already and the not yet."

This peace in the midst of inner (and outer) strife is a difficult idea for most of us to grasp. How *can* I be truly centered, mature, single-hearted when I find the contrary pull of sensuality or vanity or envy at work in me? Doesn't this other "law" indicate that I am not really sincere in my centering on the Lord? The temptation to doubt is especially strong when I find, with Paul, that "I cannot understand my own behavior. I fail to carry out the things I want to do, and I find myself doing the very things I hate" (Rom 7:15). Doesn't this contrary behavior imply that my desire for God and the good is not really sincere — and, certainly, that I am not maturing in that habit of discerning love which is the goal of our lives? It is hard to comprehend, in our own concrete experience, how Paul can be serious in the confident assurance of Romans 8.

A concrete example, which the person involved has graciously allowed me to use "in order that others might be encouraged," may help us to clarify Paul's point. Some years ago a friend came to me for direction. She was committed to a celibate life and was convinced that this was all she really desired. Yet she was

tormented, since her particular "thorn in the flesh" was unchasti-
ty. Despite a devout prayer life and a dedicated commitment to
service of others, she still did not seem able to eliminate from her
life the periodic attacks of unchaste thoughts and perhaps even
solitary actions.[2]

It was very discouraging for her, as this weakness seemed to
call into question her whole life and her very love for the Lord.
She could find psychologists, and even spiritual directors today,
who would tell her this behavior was quite normal, that there
was "nothing wrong with it." But in her heart of hearts, thank
God, she could not believe them. She knew that her love for God
required the gift of her whole self, her whole being to him. Yet
she could not give what she desired to; she did not even seem to
possess her sensual self. How could she give to the Lord what she
did not possess?

My friend's situation seemed to be a classic example of the
"two laws" of Romans 7. Yet, was it really? Like Paul she was
tormented by the fear that maybe her whole life — and her
love — was a fraud. As we shared, it occurred to me to try an
analogy. I asked her, "What is your favorite food?" Her response,
which marked her as a good Filipino, was "fried chicken." So I
said, "What would you do if you awoke tomorrow and discovered
you had lost all taste for fried chicken — if it no longer appealed to
you at all?" She replied that she would do everything possible to
recapture her taste for it, to discover why her favorite food had
lost its savor for her. "And what," I asked, "if you awoke tomorrow and discovered your unchaste temptations had disappeared
and the pull of sensuality no longer had any power over you?"
Without hesitation, she said, "I would be delighted! I think that
would be the happiest day of my life! It's what I have been praying for for many years." Since I knew her to be sincere and open,
her answer was proof enough for me that her love for the Lord
was genuine. Whatever the force of the second law in her in-
stincts, the law of the Spirit was truly at work in her heart, in her

2 In the *Dark Night of the Soul* (Book I, chapter 14), John of the Cross
says that it is not unusual for souls who have already passed through the
night of sense to be buffeted by an "angel of Satan" (cf. Paul's experience
in 2 Cor 12:7) which is "the spirit of fornication."

will. The pull of sensuality in her was quite different from her voluntary, cultivated love of fried chicken!

Recall our reason for citing this example. I was saying that one aspect of the mature habit of discerning love is an integrating peace in our lives, a centering of our lives on the Lord and a simplifying of our desires. Yet, we noted, this centering at the core of our soul can coexist with surface scattering and turmoil in our sensual nature. I would say the Paul of Romans 7 is truly centered on the Lord, despite the contrary pull of the law in his "flesh." And I would say the same of my friend, because I know something of the total pattern of her life. It is true that there are still sensual weeds in her garden whose presence is indeed frustrating to her. But the wheat *is* maturing; and, as we said in chapter 8, these weeds sometimes must be left until the Lord sees fit to uproot them.

The specific point here is that there is an interior, lasting, habitual peace in the soul, which is the mark of mature discerning love, and it can coexist with disturbance in the senses, on the surface of our lives. It is this interior peace which marks the presence of God in the dry well or dark night, once we learn to look beneath the surface of our sensible feelings. When we first enter the dark night of God's purifying love, we do not yet know any peace but that of the senses. That is, we have not learned to discriminate between what is happening in our senses and what is happening deeper in our soul. But experiences such as Paul describes in Romans 7, plus the inner darkness of the dry well, bring us to a recognition of these two distinct levels of our being. With this experiential recognition we begin to understand the "peace" which is the first gift of the Risen Lord (e.g., Lk 24:36; Jn 20:21), a peace that is not an absence of trouble, but rather a firm conviction, even and especially in the midst of turmoil, that the Lord has truly risen and "all manner of things will be well."

Integration and the Marketplace

Thus we discover that there are "levels" of consolation, one in the senses and the other deeper in the soul. The former, which was all we could perceive when we were beginners, is transitory and unreliable; it is always "with preceding cause" and so must be carefully discerned to be sure it is truly from the Lord. And even if it is, we cannot depend on it to remain with us. By contrast, the latter consolation, deeper in the soul, is a sort of abiding "consolation without preceding cause," which is God's best and surest gift to those who mature in his love. Sometimes it surfaces to consciousness — especially, perhaps, when there is conflict and turmoil at this surface level of our being: when, for example, the "law of the flesh" in us calls into question the reality of our love for God and the efficacy of his love for us. But much of the time it is a background awareness, a horizon of consciousness which animates and is incarnated in all the concrete actions of our lives. This, I believe, is what is meant, in the deepest sense, by the Ignatian phrase "contemplative in action": one who sees God in all things, yes; but, perhaps even more accurately, one who sees all things in God.[3]

We stressed from the very beginning of this book that discernment is where prayer meets action. That this is true even, and especially, when we speak of the mature habit of discerning love, is beautifully exemplified in an incident from the life of Hannah Hurnard. She is perhaps best known for her allegories of transformation in Christ, *Hinds Feet on High Places* and *Mountains of Spices*. For one who has read and loved these stories of the journey which transforms "Much Afraid" into "Grace and Glory," it is not surprising to learn that Hannah Hurnard herself is (or was) "Much Afraid." She tells us this in another book, *Wayfarer in the Land*,[4] which is the story of her missionary life in Palestine in the 1930s. She went there as part of the Christian mission to the Jews; as time passed, however, she became convinced that her real call was to the remote village dwellers and Palestinian Arabs who seemed to her the neglected outcasts of the Holy Land. She tells of the difficulties she experienced in persuading

---

3 St. Ignatius says, *"In omnibus quaerant Deum,"* "Let them seek God in all things." This is the motto of our seeking, of our *active* search for God. St. Teresa of Avila says (*Interior Castle*, Sixth Mansions, chapter 10) that one of the greatest *contemplative* gifts of God is to see all things, even one's own sinfulness, in him. Because this is pure gift, its meaning is profoundly mysterious; but I believe it is the fulfillment of the Ignatian ideal for the swimmer who has become a floater in God's sea.

4 Tyndale House, 1975, 176 pp. (originally published by Olive Press, 1951).

her superiors to allow her to work among the Arabs. When they finally agreed, the only other person who shared her desire and could be her partner in this new work was a woman whose temperament was incompatible with her own. It seemed that the only thing they had in common was their shared sense of a divine mission to the poor Arabs. Humanly speaking, it was a most unpromising partnership indeed. As Hannah Hurnard says:

> There were . . . very real divergences of opinion and temperament. And added to this was the fact, well known to both of us, that we both loved to lead and take the initiative. No wonder our friends looked askance at the idea of our working together.

And yet they felt that it was the Lord's will that they join together in this mission. For this reason,

> We decided that we would put aside one whole morning each week for prayer and for seeking the Lord's guidance and strength, and for claiming, before setting out on our visits, an open door and victory in each place we planned to go to.
> This we did. We set aside every Saturday morning for the special work of prayer and preparation. . . . We both quickly realized the value of beginning with a time of silent waiting on the Lord. In this silence we both came to him and offered ourselves to him, and became completely absorbed in his presence, asking for our minds and thoughts to be cleansed, and that we might be brought to real unity in understanding his will. Generally this silent communion with the Lord lasted about half an hour. Sometimes we were so absorbed in his presence that words would not come at all, and whole hours passed in silence. (It is not at all a question), in such times of silent communion, of making the mind a blank and waiting for ideas to come as it were "out of the blue." But rather, communion of this kind demands that every part of the mind and will be actively and joyfully handed over to the Lord for him to use. There is nothing passive about it, but the most active cooperation possible, and though at first one may feel desperately dull and heavy, and the thought of vital prayer and communion be almost impossible, the Holy Spirit invariably comes to quicken and empower, so that by the end of these mornings of prayer, we had not only listened to the Lord . . . but our minds

and bodies had also undergone a wonderful renewal of strength.[5]

If Hannah Hurnard and her companion were beginners in the interior life, several aspects of their experience might lead us to suspect that this was consolation with preceding sensible cause, and one that is quite manipulated at that: the regular, programmed schedule of Saturday morning prayer; the "claiming" from the Lord of an open door and victory (a classic expression in their evangelical tradition); the regularity with which consolation came; the stress on "the most active cooperation possible." Yet the activity described is a total handing over of one's whole being to the Lord, a waiting on him to do whatever he pleases. Even the activity of "making the mind a blank" is rejected as inappropriate, so much so that Hannah Hurnard needs to explain that the soul at such a time is not really "passive." The kind of activity she describes is indeed quite mysterious to one who has not shared her experience. But it is also strongly reminiscent of our description of "floating" as the goal of the whole experience of the dry well in prayer.[6] The floater is not passive; one who is passive will sink, not float. At the same time, the activity of the floater is quite unlike that of the swimmer. The swimmer is in control of his or her own direction and speed, whereas the floater responds to, cooperates with the wind and the current. The floater's activity is a dynamic receptivity: God is the sea in which he or she floats. Or, to vary the metaphor, God is the lead dancer and the soul is the partner completely attuned to the rhythm and pattern set by her partner. She does not lead, but neither does she hang limp like a sack of potatoes.

If we reread Hannah Hurnard's description of her experience in this light, I think her meaning becomes clear: "Communion of this kind demands that every part of the mind and will be actively and joyfully handed over to the Lord for him to use. There is nothing passive about it, but the most active cooperation possible." Like the floater or the partner in the divine dance, the soul is active but in no way manipulative. But is it suspect that

---

5 *Wayfarer in the Land*, pp. 84-86.
6 *When the Well Runs Dry*, chapter 6. See also the Epilogue of *Darkness in the Marketplace*.

"the Holy Spirit *invariably* comes to quicken and empower"? I don't think so, not in the sense Hannah Hurnard means it, and not at her level of interior maturity. It is true that St. John of the Cross spoke of the unpredictable alternation of God's presence and absence as the best sign that it is really he at work and not just our own imagination. This unpredictable, and uncontrollable alternation, however has as its purpose to teach us to "let go and let God."[7] Once we have learned the lesson, it becomes more and more "natural" to us to hand everything over to him. Then there is no reason—no obstacle in us—to prevent him from coming easily and often!

I suppose we never achieve a total letting go in this life. Hannah Hurnard implies as much when she says, "at first one may feel desperately dull and heavy, and the thought of vital prayer and communion be almost impossible." The two "laws" struggle within us as long as we live. But more and more the soul itself is given over to the law of the Spirit, and he finds almost complete freedom to lead us wherever he will. This is especially true when, as in the case of Hannah Hurnard, our prayer and our search for the Lord is apostolic. She and her companion sought him not merely for themselves, but in order that they might love one another and thereby be his effective instruments in proclaiming the Good News to the poor. This, it seems, is the most effective way to touch the heart of the God and Father of Jesus Christ. He "emptied himself" in obedience to the Father and out of love for us, and his heart goes out to those who seek to do the same for their brethren out of love for him. To them he gives the habit of discerning love: The more they have no will of their own but desire only what the Lord desires, the more they are able to "read the face of God" in knowing how he wishes them to respond to the concrete apostolic demands of their lives. Ultimately and inevitably this leads to Calvary. But that too is joy if we are there "with Christ."

Practicum Question

The culminating point of the *Spiritual Exercises* is what St.

---

7 See chapter 3 of *When the Well Runs Dry*.

Ignatius calls the "third degree (or third kind) of humility." He
says of this third degree: "Whenever the praise and glory of the
Divine Majesty would be equally served, in order to imitate and
be in reality more like Christ our Lord, I desire and choose poverty with Christ poor, rather than honors; I desire to be accounted
as worthless and a fool for Christ, rather than to be esteemed as
wise and prudent in this world. So Christ was treated before me"
(#167). Retreatants often find this frightening: To *ask for* poverty, insults, and contempt seems almost inhuman. Would our
discussion of the habit of discerning love help to see this "third
degree" of humility in a new, even joyful light?

Epilogue:
A Discerning Community

In dedicating *Opening to God* to Father Jim McCann, S.J., I mentioned that he played an important role in my own formation as a spiritual director. He had been novice master of the Philippine Jesuit province for many years, and in 1970, after I returned from graduate studies in the philosophy of science, it was he who asked that I come to San Jose Seminary to assist him in the spiritual direction of the diocesan seminarians. As Providence would have it, we only lived together for one year before he was reassigned to the Jesuit scholasticate nearby. Even then, however, he was a generous guide and an ever-ready sounding board for my problems and questions as I learned the art of spiritual direction myself. From him I learned, above all, the importance of confidentiality: that the directee, in sharing his or her inner life, invites the director into the most private and personal part of the self. It is a sacred trust and must be handled with great reverence, with a discretion and reserve approaching that of the "seal of confession" itself. On this point, Jim was firm and unyielding, and my whole experience over the years has confirmed the wisdom of his advice.

There were, however, other questions on which we did not quite see eye to eye. One such was discernment, in the sense that Jim's focus in the course he was teaching was on communal discernment whereas I, as the years passed, began to question whether this was really the proper focus or emphasis. Communal, or community, discernment was a popular and fashionable concern in the early post-Vatican II years. The democratization of religious structures, and the council-inspired reassessment of the charisms and missions of religious congregations, led to much emphasis on techniques of corporate decision making. In a faith context, this meant *discerning* God's will for the community in question, and doing it in a grass-roots, participative way that involved all the members. Since this was the thrust of charismatic communities and parish pastoral councils, as well as of religious congregations, Jim McCann's course on communal discernment was popular and well-received.

My question did not concern the essential validity of this movement in the church. In fact, I felt, and feel, that the stress on the Holy Spirit speaking in and through the faith community is one of the healthiest signs of our time. If anything, we Catholics need to move much further in this direction. One of the traditional and canonical sources of our faith is the "*pius sensus fidelium*," the "Catholic instinct (or sense) of devout believers," and yet the counter-Reformation emphasis on legitimate authority in the church has not really allowed much room for this "pious sense of believers" in the development of doctrine in response to the concrete demands of the times. Since Vatican II there has been a widespread effort to remedy this deficiency, an effort which has borne much fruit, despite the inevitable (and perennial) problems involved in balancing authority and discernment in the church.[1]

What, then, was my question concerning Father McCann's course on communal discernment? I felt that the real problem in discernment is not at the communal but at the *personal* level. That is, to have a discerning community you must have discerning persons, discerning members of the community. And to be a discerning person you need to be a praying person. Discernment is, as we have stressed throughout this book, a function of one's personal relationship to God. It is where prayer meets action; the more deeply one knows the Lord, the easier it will be to "read his face" and to sense what he desires us to do. Thus it is dangerous to speak of communal discernment if the members of the community in question are not, individually, praying and discerning persons.

This was my feeling back in 1975, and I sensed that Jim McCann agreed with me in principle. Despite his much greater experience and wisdom, he encouraged me to question and he ex-

---

1 We discussed the basic principles of this delicate balance in chapter 3 of *Opening to God*. See also chapter 1 above.

plored my doubts with me. He was, however, a sick man and by February of 1977 he was dead. At that point he presented me with my greatest challenge; the course on discernment became mine to teach and I had to think seriously about implementing the ideas and doubts we had been sharing. As the whole thrust of this book makes clear—since it is only in this Epilogue that we come to discuss communal discernment—my convictions about the central focus of discernment have been confirmed and strengthened during the intervening years.

Many people today express well-grounded misgivings about community discernment, and even feel uncomfortable with the word, "discernment." It can easily be a polite and pious name for a "tyranny of the majority," a way of attaching the Lord's name and authority to what most of the group want, or believe he must want. If this happens, then, as we have seen, "discernment" becomes a way of manipulating God to agree with our (perhaps sincere) convictions concerning action and decision making. If, however, the prerequisites and qualities of genuine discernment, as described in chapter 3 above, are present in the individual members of the discerning community—if, that is, they are sincere and committed pray-ers who are open to discover God's will, and who realize the limitations of any faith-discernment as we have described them—then the "mechanics" of communal discernment are easy enough to learn and to implement.

The classic paradigm for communal discernment is the famous Deliberation of 1539, when the first companions of St. Ignatius Loyola deliberated concerning God's will for them and discerned that he wished them to form the religious community to be known as The Society of Jesus. Of the many recent analyses of the process they followed, I have found most helpful that of John Carroll Futrell, S.J., *Communal Discernment: Reflections on Experience.*[2] Futrell outlines seven steps which emerge from an analysis of this paradigmatic experience of communal discernment. And he describes several variations of procedure which

---

2 *Studies in the Spirituality of Jesuits*, volume IV, #5 (November, 1972). Futrell gives several other recent references, especially in footnotes 1 and 16. Cf. also the selected bibliography in Jules Toner's *A Commentary on St. Ignatius' Rules for the Discernment of Spirits* (pp. 315-318), the Institute of Jesuit Sources, 1982.

may be employed in diverse situations.

The basic approach is similar to our description (in chapter 4) of St. Ignatius' third "time" or occasion for making a good choice. Once the necessary data has been gathered and the question to be discerned has been clearly formulated,[3] the process involves alternating periods of prayer and sharing of insights on the pros and cons of the question. Finally, each member of the community withdraws to pray and to seek a sense (by means of the rules for consolation and desolation described in chapters 5 to 7 above) of the Lord's will in the matter at hand. If, when they return together to share their personal discernments, there is "unanimity" concerning the Lord's will, then the community discernment has been valid and fruitful.

Prerequisites for Communal Discernment

Futrell's monograph discusses several important questions that may arise. What, for example, do we mean by "unanimity" of discernment in this context? What of an individual member who discerns differently from the rest of the community? Would her contrary discernment invalidate the process? Or would it be a sign that she had not discerned properly? Or that she was called to be a prophet in the community? Futrell explores the possibilities and gives wise guidelines for answering the questions raised. He says, for example, that the unanimity in question is not "in the head" but "in the heart." That is, it is not a unanimity of opinions or ideas, but a shared *felt* sense that this is God's word to this community at this point in its history. It is the feelings we discern; and here, as in personal discernment, one can *feel* that something is God's will without *understanding* why. As we have noted, Gethsemane is the supreme example of this *faith*-sensitivity to what pleases our God.

Of particular interest to us is Futrell's discussion of the prerequisites of communal discernment. In chapter 3, we spoke

---

3 Futrell makes the wise suggestion that the question be one that can be answered "Yes" or "No": for example, "Shall we close St. Vitus School?" or "Should we (Ed and Maria) get a divorce?" Such a clearly focused question is much more likely to be fruitfully discerned than a vague one like "What shall we do about St. Vitus?" or "What does the Lord want of us (Ed and Maria)?"

of certain prerequisites for *all* discernment, and Futrell recognizes their importance when members of a community gather to discern the Lord's will for the group. But, he says, there are other prerequisites for this specific communal situation:

> Now, a community can engage in a process of authentic communal spiritual discernment only if certain prerequisites are fulfilled on the *community* level, even if the individual members of the community (or at least a significant majority of them) have already fulfilled the *sine qua non* condition that they are praying and truly discerning individually. It is vital, then, that a community honestly identify where it actually is with respect to fulfilling these prerequisites (p. 167).

Futrell lists three such preconditions for an authentic and fruitful communal discernment. If they are lacking, he says, then the community may merely be united by "a corporate awareness of shared pain and frustration." In this case communal discernment is not presently possible; "starting from where it is, however, the community, by identifying both the positive and negative dynamics at work in the causes of the pain and frustration, can begin to move consciously toward growth in fulfilling the prerequisites of communal spiritual discernment. Here, the help of the techniques of contemporary group dynamics can be a valuable aid."

What are these essential prerequisites for authentic communal discernment? Futrell enumerates three, the first of which is "communion," a sharing in a common charism or a "common vocation from the Holy Spirit." For Christians in general this would be a common faith in Jesus Christ as the Lord and model of our lives; for Jesuits, a common sense that we are "sons" of St. Ignatius Loyola and that this sonship, by the grace of God, defines our mission and lifestyle and community in a special way. Similarly, for members of a parish community it would be a faith conviction that the Lord has called us together to *be* "church" in a visible way at this place and time.

Symbols play an important part, in every case, in expressing and deepening this sense of communion. As Rosemary Haughton has shown in her classic book, *The Transformation of Man* (London: Geoffrey Chapman, 1967), the symbolic, "liturgical" dimension of a community's life together provides the "formative" framework within which transforming encounter can take place. Without this formative or formational dimension, genuine communion of life and vision will not be possible. And, as Futrell notes, we live in an age when many of the "shared non-verbal symbols" of our communion have broken down. Structures of religious community life, identifying styles of dress, even life together in one house—in many religious communities, none of these shared non-verbal symbols has the same power to form and embody genuine "communion" as it had in the past. Similarly, the increased mobility of modern urbanized lay life tends to break down the stable structures of the past: People move much more frequently today, from neighborhood to neighborhood and even from city to city; and even when they "stay put," their place of work (and even of recreation) is often far removed from where they live. In general, the familiar structures which provide the formational climate for transforming encounter, the shared non-verbal symbols of small-town or closed-community life, are no longer such a prominent part of our lives.

Is this bad? Not necessarily; but it does make more difficult that "consciously shared experience of profound union in a common vocation"—the shared core experience of a common charism—which Futrell sees as the first prerequisite for community discernment. For this reason, his second prerequisite becomes all the more essential. It is, he says, "common agreement on the basic expression of this communion in words here and now." That is, we must not only share a common charism, which is the touchstone of every specific discernment; in addition, we must be able to agree on a "basic verbal expression" of this charism. For example, it will not be enough for a community of Jesuits to share their "jesuitness" if they cannot verbalize in some mutually acceptable way what it means to be a Jesuit.

This does not mean they will agree on every detail of this Jesuit identity. They may, in fact, have very different ideas about the appropriate concrete application of their charism in a given historical and social situation. In fact, John Cogley is supposed to have said that "Every little movement has a Jesuit all its own," a clever saying which, in my experience, is very close to the truth!

Yet, diverse as we are, we Jesuits can and do agree on certain basics. Most fundamental, perhaps, is that a Jesuit is one formed by the *Spiritual Exercises* of St. Ignatius, and one thereby committed to the Ignatian "magis," the search for the *greater* glory of God which dominated St. Ignatius' own life—and this in a community of sinful men for whom Ignatius himself is the ideal Jesuit. This, at least, is the way I, after 34 years as a Jesuit, would begin to formulate in words what makes me a Jesuit. Futrell's point is that I could not begin to discern with my brother-Jesuits concerning the concrete living of our Jesuit life today, unless we could agree upon this, or some, expression of what makes us Jesuits.

Similarly, *any* community, lay or religious, would need this shared verbal expression of their charism as the touchstone for their communal discernment today. Otherwise they would not have any basis, any point of reference for their community discernment. Their discussions would end in radical confusion—and even acrimony—if they did not have a common basic commitment as the norm of their specific choices. Thus it is important that any community which hopes to discern together God's will for them be agreed upon the core vision which makes them a community in the first place. What is their reason for being a community? What defining goal and values do they share? As Futrell says,

> The verbal expression used to express the communion will vary at different moments in history, as the meaning of all expression does. An individual person may feel that he could compose a more beautiful expression than the one agreed upon. The important thing, however, is that all the members of the community together can recognize in the words (chosen) *a* basic expression of their underlying communion, so that they can use it together as the norm of all their communal discernment (p. 169).

The third prerequisite for community discernment cited by Futrell is equally essential: "Common commitment to carrying out the decisions reached through communal discernment." This may sound simple, but it is really the most difficult of the three. It implies giving the Holy Spirit a "blank check" *prior* to the deliberations, committing ourselves in advance to whatever he desires, provided only we can be sure it is his desire. Many of us, as we noted earlier in speaking of the climate of discernment, would like to know God's will before we decide whether to follow it. We ask him to tell us what he would like, and only then will we decide upon our response. At times, especially when dealing with less mature and less committed pray-ers, the Lord can and does adapt to our demands here. But such an attitude is a sign of weak faith and limited trust. We are not really sure whether we can safely entrust our lives to the Lord. What if he asks something too difficult or too costly? And even when he does accommodate himself to our fragile faith, he cannot really work with full freedom and power in us, since we reserve the ultimate decision — and control — to ourselves.

To fruitfully discern, then, a community must, as Futrell says,

> be truly committed beforehand to living out the election to which the Holy Spirit moves them through their communal discernment: to execute it no matter what the cost, individually or corporately. If this essential "Ignatian indifference"[4] is lacking there is no point in beginning to discern together. The community is seeking to discern the actual word of God to it as a community here and now, and all must be totally open to the Spirit, so that they can say "Yes, Father" together, even to a disconcerting and unexpected word (p. 169).

I think it is clear why I have said that this third prerequisite is the most difficult to realize. It is rare enough to find an individual soul with this radical openness to God. How much more difficult to find a whole community thus open and "indifferent"!

---

4 Futrell's comment brings out clearly the correct meaning of "indifference," an essential but much misunderstood aspect of any genuine holiness. In ordinary language, to be indifferent connotes not caring, lacking interest and zest. But the religious indifference of which St. Ignatius (with many other saints) speaks is quite different. It is, like St. John of the Cross' freedom or detachment from our (disordered) desires (*Ascent of Mount Carmel*, Book I), a function of a passionate caring. A man who truly loves his wife may well be indifferent to all other women, not because he is sick or apathetic, but because he cares so passionately for one woman. Similarly religious indifference implies that God is so all-important to us that every other value pales in comparison with his love.

This is perhaps the main reason why we have discovered in recent years that genuine communal discernment is difficult and not very common. It would imply that every member of the community was single-minded and single-hearted in his or her desire for God's will. Rare as this disposition is, however, the effort to achieve it — and the experience of our failure — can be very salutary. The first step toward becoming free for God is the realization of how unfree we are. Once we do realize this experientially and can accept the humbling truth of our realization, then the good Lord can begin to lead us, individually and as a community, out of our slavery to our attachments and into the land of freedom.

"Set My People Free"

As we come to the end of our consideration of discernment in Christian life, this stress on genuine freedom of spirit forms a beautiful *leitmotif* for the whole discussion. Freedom is both a precondition and the greatest fruit of a life of discerning love. Maybe this is why, according to St. Ignatius, we always discern only "to some extent," more accurately as we mature, but never (in this life) with full clarity and certainty, because we are never totally free, totally open to God. In fact, the more we grow, the more painfully aware of our unfreedom we become.

In the beginning, the tiny shoots of the wheat and the weeds are virtually indistinguishable. But as the wheat matures, and the weeds along with it, the difference between the two becomes more and more evident. At the same time, as we noted in chapter 8, it becomes clearer that some of these weeds are beyond our power to uproot. We now recognize them as weeds, and our greatest desire is to present a good harvest to the Lord, but we find we are not really free to uproot the most persistent of the unwanted weeds. In fact, the Lord himself tells us that they must be allowed to grow until the harvest when he will make the final separation.

Despite this enduring lack of full freedom to love and to respond to love, it nonetheless remains true that the surest sign of maturing in discerning love is a growth in freedom of spirit. St.

John of the Cross, in the third stanza of *The Living Flame of Love*,[5] has a beautiful discussion of the three great enemies of interior growth. As a spiritual director I try to reread this section every year, since John's third enemy of growth, besides the devil and oneself, is the spiritual director! He spends a few paragraphs each on the devil and the self, after devoting, ironically, almost 30 paragraphs to the director as an obstacle to growth. Why? Because, he says, most directors do not really free their directees to grow. That is, they themselves lack the inner freedom to allow their directees to follow wherever the Spirit may lead them. Most directors, John feels, try to form carbon copies of themselves: If they have found fruit in devotion to the Holy Shroud, then all of their directees must also be "shroudites." They are true directors (in the sense that they actively direct others' lives) rather than genuine co-discerners.

Many good souls, it would seem, prefer to be directed in this sense. They find security in blindly entrusting themselves into the hands of another. But the problem is that they never grow, they do not become discerning, sensitive lovers themselves. And this is why St. John of the Cross says that directors who "direct" are great enemies of growth. Despite their good will, they do not foster that genuine inner freedom which is the fruit of growth in discerning love. They themselves are slaves to a "cookbook" of spirituality, and their disciples become slaves either to the same cookbook or to the director as the authentic interpreter of that cookbook. There is no room for the Divine Chef to exercise his creativity in them, to engage them in a dialogue of love which is utterly unique and personal.

I try to reread this passage from John of the Cross every year because it forms a reminder and a check for me. The ultimate test of my effectiveness as a director is the growing freedom of spirit of my directees. It seems the same could be said of a religious superior, or a parent. In every case, the goal is, in a sense, to "put yourself out of business." That is, we seek to form mature and responsible persons who can stand on their own: men and women who have interiorized the external structures and who can live by

---

5 The paragraph numbering differs in John's two versions of the *Flame*, but the section referred to is, in the revised version, paragraphs 29 to 67.

the inner law of love. This, in the end, is the real meaning of a life of discerning love. As we said, it is almost never achieved fully and perfectly in this life. But it is the goal of our striving and of this book.

St. Paul says there is no law for those who are reborn in Christ Jesus; St. Augustine says, "Love and do what you wish"; and St. Teresa of Avila gives as the only norm for prayer, "Do whatever most moves you to love." If you and I can better understand now what Paul and Augustine and Teresa really mean, then these pages have been fruitful, for the writer and for the reader.

Appendix:
The Practicum Questions

At the conclusion of each chapter, a practicum question was suggested for your reflection. As I said at the end of chapter 1, I have found these questions helpful to the students in assimilating the matter in my course on discernment, particularly since discernment is an art, a practical art, which is learned by doing. Similarly, at the end of each week's lecture my students are given the practicum question for that week. They reflect upon it during the weekend and write up their answer. The first hour of our next session, they meet in small groups to share and discuss their answers to the questions. I sit in on one of the groups, but try to remain in the background, to listen and perhaps make some notes concerning points that need clarification or insights which might be helpful to the whole class. Then, at the beginning of the next hour's lecture on the new matter, I give my own "answer" to the question proposed.

Since this format seems to have been very helpful for my students, I have included similar practicum questions at the end of each chapter of this book; and I will now offer my own response to the questions asked. It is important to note, however, that frequently there is no single correct solution to the cases or questions proposed. What I can share with my students, and with you, is the fruit of my own experience and reflection. But there may be other ways of viewing the question or handling the problem. For this reason, in my course I collect the written answers to the practicum question before offering my own solution, and read and comment upon each paper before the next lecture. There may be various approaches to a given practical problem, as is also true in scientific experimentation or in medical diagnosis. What is important is that the beginning discerner develop a good feel for the data provided, a sense of what questions need to be asked, and a consistent, perceptive approach in weighing and evaluating the facts uncovered. In a real sense, a good discerner is much like a good detective, sorting the evidence and centering on that which is essential. It is not an easy art, as we have seen, since what is essential is often "invisible to the eye." Let us see, though, whether my comments can help us to focus on the "invisible essential."

Chapter 1: Signs of Authentic Prophecy

Our first question dealt with the six criteria for authentic prophecy, drawn from the Old Testament and discussed in chapter 1. Which of these six would you consider most helpful in discerning a genuine prophet *today*? While the first two—predicting misfortune rather than good fortune, and predicting "signs" which do come to pass—would still be valid and useful, I would not consider them the most helpful criteria. It is true even today that people are more receptive to someone who tells them the good news they want to hear, than to a "prophet of doom." Thus a false prophet, who is using his "gift" to gain power and popularity, would be more likely to pander to the vanity and self-centeredness of his hearers. But bad news *alone* would not be a very solid sign of authentic prophesy. Some audiences have a perverted desire for self-flagellation; with them, a dishonest prophet would do well (if not good!) to gain power and influence by proclaiming the misfortune they perversely desire.

Similarly, as we saw in chapter 7, the devil himself can work wonders—even pious wonders—to accomplish his own ends. It is true that Jesus appeals to his "signs" (especially in St. John's gospel) as a basis for belief in him. But false prophets, from the time of Elijah to the early church of Acts, also performed signs and wonders to gain attention and acceptance. Moreover, miracles are not a very common phenomenon in our day; as far as I can recall, none of the figures mentioned in the practicum question (Gandhi, Martin Luther King, Pope John XXIII) was known to have worked miracles in confirmation of his prophetic mission.

The fifth and sixth criteria—the prophet's intention and own personal experience of a prophetic call from God—are surely very important to the prophet himself or herself. The problem is that they are *interior* criteria, not directly observable or able to be experienced by anyone but the prophet in question. It seems they would be of little help to you or me in judging the authenticity of someone else, since we cannot enter into the heart and soul of the purported prophet. We can only judge by what we see. Note, however, that we are not judging the sincerity of the prophet in question; as the Lord Jesus has insisted, this is really none of our business. What we are judging — and must judge if we are to follow or reject the call of such a prophet discerningly — is whether his or her claim to be the mouthpiece of God for us is genuine, and thus whether we should follow the call to act or respond in a certain way.

We are left, then, with the third and the fourth criteria: the test of fidelity to the basic doctrine of "Israel" (i.e., for us, to the revelation confirmed and perfected by Jesus Christ) and the life witness of the prophet, his or her credibility as a living embodiment of Christ's own passion for God. In my judgment, both of these would be most helpful in evaluating a contemporary prophet. After much reflection on my own experience as a discerner and a co-discerner, I think I would give greater weight to the former criterion, the fidelity of the prophet to the revelation of "Israel." It seems to me somewhat more objective than the life witness criterion. For example, questions have been raised about the personal moral life of Martin Luther King, questions which I, at least, could not answer with certainty. Yet, it seems to me that the essential and consistent Christianity of his message is a very strong argument in favor of his genuine prophetic role for our times. Would I be surer, and happier, if the few doubts raised about his moral life could be resolved in his favor? Of course. But discernment is not infallible; it is only "to some extent," and the third and fourth criteria would seem to me to be most helpful in making such a judgment about Martin Luther King, or any contemporary "prophet."

Chapter 2: Jesus and John Discerning

There were two practicum questions for this chapter. The

first concerned Jesus' own "infallible" discernment of his person and mission: Would Jesus' unique discernment have any practical relevance to my own life of discernment? I believe it would. Recall that we defined "infallible" as unerring. That is, we took it to mean that Jesus was unerringly guided by the Holy Spirit in his discernment of the Father's will precisely because he was totally open to that will, even though he, like us, had to discover where the Father was leading him in his human life. In Jesus' life, the prerequisites of genuine discernment (discussed in chapter 3) were perfectly realized: He gave the Spirit a "blank check" to lead him wherever the Father desired.

Most of us can never be as totally open to the Lord in this life as Jesus was. Yet his example is of paramount importance to us, both as a model and as a source of encouragement. He was "tempted in every way that we are" and still he did not sin. He knows our human condition from the inside. He is Emmanuel, God-with-us. Nothing could be such a source of strength and encouragement to us, in our human pilgrimage, as the realization that we have a God who chose to experience fully our struggle to live by faith in the midst of darkness. Moreover, his life of discerning love is a model, an ideal for us, and because he was truly one of us, it is an *attainable* ideal. The devil will do everything possible to push our God off into the distant clouds, to make him so unattainably holy that he seems irrelevant to our real human trials and weaknesses. In fact, this satanic idea has had considerable vogue in our century: God is often seen as an oppressive, demanding tyrant who must be eliminated if man is to be fully human. Yet, if one is truly aware of what it means that Jesus, living and loving and learning like us, is the "sacrament" of God's redemptive love for all people, then God will never be experienced as distant and oppressive. He is the all-holy One indeed; but in Jesus we discover that we are called to be, and can become, like him, not by our own efforts but by the same gift of grace by which Jesus was "constituted Son in glory because of his obedience." In St. Augustine's beautiful words, "God became man in order that man might become God." What could be more "practical" than this hope and this example, which is the manna for our own journey? "Let us be confident then, in approaching the throne of grace, that we shall have mercy from him and find grace when we are in need of help" (Heb 4:16).

Our second practicum question concerned the discernment of John the Baptist. If you could meet him, what question(s) would you like to ask him about his discernment, either of his own mission or of the person and mission of Jesus? For me, the scriptural references to John's ministry raise many questions. For example, if he was truly the cousin of Jesus, as St. Luke's gospel tells us, why did he say in St. John's gospel (1:31-34) that he did not know Jesus until the Spirit pointed him out, especially if he leapt in the womb of Elizabeth at the time of the visitation? Again, how did he understand his own baptism in relation to that of Jesus? Was John really an Essene, a member of the Qumran community which we have come to know through the Dead Sea Scrolls? Is this the background of his own messianic expectations by which he judged the ministry of Jesus?

But the one question which I would most like to ask John the Baptist—because of its relevance to my own experience of discernment—would be concerning his famous "doubt" in Matthew 11 (v. 2-6). It has been said traditionally that John himself did not really doubt Jesus' messiahship, that he sent the disciples to question Jesus in order that their own faith might be strengthened. But Matthew's narrative gives no hint of this. Taken at face value, it would clearly imply that John the Baptist himself underwent a real dark night of doubt: It would seem that Jesus was not acting as John had expected him to, and that John really wondered whether his whole ministry had been a mistake.[1] He was in prison, about to die for his beliefs; it would certainly be desolating to suspect that one was dying for a mistake!

The reason I would wish to ask John about his real feelings at this time is because his experience—and Jesus' reply to the questioning disciples—could be very important for us. As we see in

---

1 There is a hint of this in Jesus' discourse to the crowds after the departure of John's disciples. Jesus contrasts John's austere, "prophetic" lifestyle with his own; he says that (11:19) "the son of Man came, eating and drinking, and they say, 'Look, a glutton and a drunkard, a friend of tax collectors and sinners!' " Since John came "neither eating nor drinking," Jesus' lifestyle may well have contradicted his expectations of what the Messiah would be like.

chapter 3, our discernment is almost always tentative and reform-able. We discern, as St. Ignatius says, "to some extent," and the final test of our discernment is in the living of the choice we thus make. If John really doubted, the same commitment in the obscurity of faith would be seen in his life. And Jesus' answer to John — the "signs" of healing, concern for the poor, trust to which he appeals (11:4-6) — would also be his answer to us in the dark moments of living our own life of discerning love. I do believe that John really doubted, and that Jesus' appeal to his signs was really his greatest tribute to the total faith of his precursor. But it would be very good, very reassuring to hear that this was so from the lips of John himself.

Chapter 3: Discernment in My Own Life

Chapter 3 treated the place of discernment in our own lives today. We spoke especially of the "climate" of discernment: the prerequisites and the essential qualities of heart for any genuine and fruitful discernment of God's will in a concrete life situation. Since the practicum question asked you to describe some specific discernment situation in your own life, I cannot really give a general answer to the question. You might wish, though, to check the case you described to see whether it is properly focused.

Is it, first, a good case for discernment? That is, is it suffi-ciently important to warrant discernment? And is it really a case or situation in which God's will is unclear? Sometimes, as we shall see, we seek to discern because we don't want to decide. This can happen, for example, when people ask me to help them discern whether they have a religious or priestly vocation. In itself, this is certainly a valid matter for discernment. But at times I find, as I listen to and share with the directee, that God's will is already quite clear; what is lacking is the courage and faith to act on what he is asking.

If the situation you recalled from your own experience is suf-ficiently important and sufficiently unclear to warrant discern-ment, then you might next check whether it is clearly focused on the precise matter to be discerned. Discernment is ordered to ac-tion, it is the meeting point of prayer and concrete response to God's word. Letty is asking whether she should align herself with the "activist" group in the community; Joe wants to know whether he should remain in the seminary or leave temporarily to help his needy family; Ed and Maria have to choose between staying together or separating for the sake of the children. Is your own discernment question equally clear-cut and specific? If the question is too vague, or if there are several questions all jumbled together, it will be very difficult to discern fruitfully. In the Epilogue we see examples of this with respect to communal discernment.

The question also asked which of the prerequisites and essential qualities of genuine discernment you find most lacking in yourself. This application of the three prerequisites and three essential qualities to your own personal situation can be a fruitful "consciousness examen." Self-knowledge is a crucial foundation, not only for discernment but for any genuine interior life. And since it is not always easy to see ourselves as we truly are, it could be helpful to check your self-evaluation by asking a friend or director who knows the "inner you" how he or she sees you. Which of the qualities and prerequisites does that person feel you lack or are weak in? The answer might be quite revealing.

Chapter 4: Advising Sister Letty

Since chapter 4 discusses St. Ignatius' three times or occasions for making a good choice, our practicum question asked how you would begin to advise Sister Letty, whom we met in chapter 3. She is the young sister who had just pronounced her first vows and was unsure about the stand she should take on social-political activism. As I hope is clear by now, it would be a great mistake to advise her, when she first presents her problem to you, either to leave the congregation *or* to simply obey superiors and stop questioning. You might conceivably be giving her good advice — sharing with her *your* prudent opinion about the matter — but you would be failing as a co-discerner, an interpreter of what the Lord is saying to *her*. Assuming that God's will is not clear and unambiguous (as would be the case, for example, if one of the alternatives she is considering is clearly sinful), then your task is to help her listen to her own feelings and to interpret what the Lord might be asking by means of these feelings.

In chapters 5, 6 and 7 we explore how to interpret our feelings as signs of God's will, but even here in chapter 4 we can see already that it would not be wise to bypass her feelings and simply tell her what to do. Neither would it be wise, as the second part of the question proposes, to *immediately* suggest to her one of St. Ignatius' two methods for a "third (or reasoning) time" decision. We have seen that this third time is a time of "tranquillity," when God seems silent and our feelings do not give us any guidance in determining his will. In Sister Letty's case, as described, it seems quite unlikely that there would be no feelings to discern!

In any case, however, we can presume the "first (or revelation) time" clarity of a Paul or a Matthew is not Sister Letty's experience. But we should check on what happens when she brings the question to prayer. If there are diverse movements of "spirits," such as those Ignatius mentions in describing the second time, then we have matter for discernment and will have to apply the rules discussed in the next three chapers.

Only if there are no such feelings reported by Sister Letty can we turn to Ignatius' third time methods for coming to a decision about God's will. Hence we should *begin* with Sister Letty by simply allowing her to share her whole experience. Has she prayed over it? If so, what answer does she seem to receive from the Lord? If there are conflicting inspirations at different times, then we have the raw material for discernment proper (Ignatius' second time), and can use the rules to be discussed in the following chapters. If there are no inspirations or movements of the "spirits," then we may suggest to Sister Letty St. Ignatius' methods for the third time.

Chapter 5: The Fundamental Option and Our Feelings

Chapter 5 introduced us to St. Ignatius' rules for discernment. While the section discussed is from the first week rules, it really treats of the basic states of soul which are relevant to all discernment. Two principal points were stressed: the importance of our "fundamental option" in determining the tactics of God and of the evil spirit and the meaning of the two feeling states, consolation and desolation, which are the raw material of all discernment. The practicum question asks you to reflect on both of these basic points as revealed in your own experience.

First, can you be sure that your own fundamental option is "for God," so that consolation would properly be his voice and desolation the voice of the evil spirit? In effect this would mean: Do I have living faith? And we know from scripture and the church's tradition that we can never be absolutely certain that we are in the state of grace, of living faith. We believe, we hope that we are in grace; but in this life, barring an extraordinary gift of God which would be an anticipation of heaven, we "work out our salvation in fear and trembling." This is not a cause for alarm; it is merely the essential meaning of living by faith and not by clear vision. Moreover, we possess "signs," tangible clues that we do live in the grace and love of our God. Our desire for him and to please him is itself such a sign; we cannot even desire him, or desire to do his will, unless grace is at work in our lives. And a constant, long-lasting desire to live in his love would be a very good sign that we are "in grace." This desire, of course, will in turn manifest itself in concrete ways — our sensitivity to the needs of others, our growth in trust in the face of difficult trials, all the "flowers" we discussed in chapter 2 of *When the Well Runs Dry*.

The second part of this practicum question asked whether you find it easy to recognize and "name" your own feelings. This is especially difficult for people who have been raised to repress or suppress their real feelings. I have lived in only two cultures, the Filipino and the American and, different as they are in many ways, I would say that there is much repression of feeling in both. American boys don't cry. Filipinos, boys or girls, don't do or say anything which will make them singular; they conform to the expectations of the group (*pakikisama*) in ways which discourage both crime and excellence. Having directed at least a few people from several other cultures, I have come to believe that it is not easy for *any* of us human beings to be truly in touch with our own real feelings. I know, for myself, that the longer I live the more mysterious I find myself, and my own reactions to persons and events. It is true that, if we really mature, we do come to a deeper self-knowledge. As that happens we are better equipped to discern. But a healthy self-doubt should also be an important fruit of that maturing. That is why spiritual direction — the objective view of one who can see us "from the outside" — will always be valuable for souls committed to growth.

Chapter 6: Job's Desolation and Ours

We asked two questions concerning desolation at the end of this chapter. The first was to decide which of the three reasons for desolation would apply to the hero of the Book of Job, and the second was to recall some significant desolation experience of your own and to reflect on how well you handled it in the light of the rules given in chapter 6. Concerning the latter, it is important to recall that desolation is a normal and healthy part of any solid faith life. If anyone told me he or she had never experienced any significant desolation, I would feel sure that the person was either leading a very sheltered "hothouse" life or else, more likely, was not really in touch with his or her own feelings. At the same time that desolation is quite normal, however, it is also true that we usually do not handle it very gracefully until we have had long schooling in the dry well or the dark night.

The experience of Job is instructive and consoling here. He was, as we have seen, an outstanding servant of Yahweh — in the judgment of the Lord himself, the best on the face of the earth. Yet, when Satan was permitted to try him by desolation, Job was devastated by the experience. Fortunately, he could not accept the advice of his friends to surrender blindly to the apparently harsh judgment of God and to confess a sin of which he was not aware. But he did conclude, mistakenly, that his God had abandoned him. And he begged the Lord, at one point, to simply kill him and get it over with.

Job's desolation was not due to his own negligence or sinfulness. We, the readers, know this from the very beginning of the story. Job also believes it, and yet, why is he suffering? The author tells us in chapter 1 that God permits Satan to test him in order to prove his love and his fidelity — to prove that Job is not just a fair-weather friend of Yahweh. As the story progresses, though, we begin to realize that this is not merely a test of Job's *present* state of soul. Whatever Satan may have intended, the trial becomes the purifying fire in which Job's love is refined and made stronger than death. By the end of the book, Job can say to God: "I have been holding forth on matters I cannot understand, on marvels beyond me and my knowledge. . . . I knew you then only by hearsay; but now, having seen you with my own eyes, I retract all I have said" (42:3,5). This is a beautiful example of St. Ignatius' second reason why God may permit desolation: to "test our love as steel is tested by fire."

The third reason of Ignatius — to teach us that everything, every consolation is pure gift, which we cannot merit or manipulate — is not so evident in the story of Job. I do believe, though, that in reality the second and the third reasons usually go together. That is, for committed, devout souls desolation both teaches them to let go and float, and, at the same time, purifies and transforms their love. The desire and instinct to control our lives is, in fact, probably the most important and deepest-rooted "impurity" in us.

There is, perhaps, a hint of this in the later chapters of the Book of Job. Beginning in chapter 38, God says to Job, "All right. You have questioned me enough. Now it is my turn to question you." And he proceeds to enumerate the wonders of creation — the stars in the heavens, Leviathan in the Mediterranean Sea, the mountain goat giving birth — asking repeatedly: "How did these wonders come to be? Since you know so much, explain them to me." The point is gently and lovingly ironic: "Since you, Job, know so little of the mysteries of the universe, how can you presume to understand my ways of dealing with you? How can you conclude that I have abandoned and rejected you?" Even the meaning of Job's sufferings is beyond his power of comprehension or manipulation. Everything, even Job's purifying trial, is gift.

Chapter 7: Biblical Consolations

In chapter 7 we discussed the delicate art of discerning consolation. As we saw, consolation without preceding cause could only be from God himself. It is less common than consolation with preceding sensible cause, but when it occurs it is surely from the Lord. Of the consolations mentioned in the practicum question, the joy of the blind man upon receiving his sight (Lk 18:43) and of Zacchaeus when Jesus called him down from the tree (Lk

19:6), both seem to be "with preceding cause." While there is no sign of the tail of the snake in either experience—the beginning, middle and end of both all appear to be good—in each case the cause of the consolation is the sensible, healing encounter with Jesus Christ. Thus the consolations of Zacchaeus and the blind man would be genuine consolations *with* a preceding sensible cause.

By contrast, the story of the multiplication of the loaves in John 6 (v. 1-15) clearly reveals the tail of the snake. Again there is consolation in the crowd's acclamation that Jesus is the "prophet," the Messiah (6:14), and again there is a preceding sensible cause, the miraculous multiplication of the loaves and fish by which Jesus fed them. But there is a hint of trouble in the concluding verse (6:15), when John says that Jesus perceived they were "about to come and take him *by force* and make him king." While the miracle was genuine enough and was truly the work of Jesus, the "end" of the experience does not appear to be good. The evil spirit must have insinuated himself into the work of God. That this was indeed so is confirmed by Jesus' words to the crowd when they finally catch up with him on the other side of the sea (6:26-27). Their "faith," he tells them, was not genuine: They sought him not because of his "signs" but because their bellies were filled with bread.

Finally, the experience of Peter at the end of the same chapter appears to be a genuine consolation without sensible cause. The whole chapter, the "eucharistic discourse," has been a series of challenges to the faith of Jesus' prospective disciples. Gradually they have drifted away, unable to accept the faith demands of his teaching, until finally only the Twelve remain. When Jesus asks them, "Do you want to go away too?" Peter is the one to reply: "Lord, who shall we go to? You have the message of eternal life, and we believe." Peter's strong faith is especially beautiful because it appears to be without any preceding cause in the senses. In fact, all the sensible causes—the conflict with the crowd and the Pharisees, Jesus' strong and puzzling words, the turning away of virtually all his hearers—would be more likely to produce desolation in Peter. He reflects this when he asks, "Lord, who shall we go to?" He doesn't understand Jesus any better than the others did; but he believes and trusts him, *despite* all the desolating sensible circumstances.

Chapter 8: The Weeds of Today

Our practicum question for chapter 8 asked which of the weeds we have discussed—the world, the flesh, and the devil—would grow most abundantly in the Lord's harvest field today. I suppose we have to say, now as always, that *all* three varieties are alive and flourishing. The values of the "world," of the secular culture within which the soul is planted, vary from age to age and from place to place. But they are always a problem for the committed follower of Christ. Our age values science and success and the hard work of the self-made man, at least if we belong to the cultures of the first world. All of these are goods, but they can easily be exaggerated to the point where there is little room left for God and faith. In this regard, the capitalist first world and the Marxist second world can be very strange bedfellows indeed: Despite their radically different perspectives on the way society should be organized, both can easily exalt man and woman to the point where the divine dimension of our lives is either irrelevant or a dangerous obstacle to a person's self-perfectibility. In the third world, the problem may be different. Given the poverty and frustration which is the daily lot of so many, a utopian view of humanity may not be so appealing. But this does not necessarily mean that the culture, the third "world," is more hospitable to true faith. Superstition, fatalism and the tendency to blame all my troubles on someone else (or some impersonal institution) can be equally noxious weeds in the Lord's garden.

As for the flesh, the self-love and sensuality of the instinctual side of us, I suppose no one needs proof that this weed is flourishing today. The "let it all hang out," "do your own thing," "look out for number one," ethos of today has infected almost every society. Following one's feelings wherever they lead is not only fashionable but "scientifically" respectable. Self-control and stable commitment and fidelity are not fashionable; frequently, in fact, they are not even considered humanly possible. While I would be one of the few, perhaps, who feel that the lure of the flesh is no greater today than in earlier, more repressive ages, and that it is at least doubtful whether permissiveness is any more unhealthy in the end than the socially-imposed prudery of the past, there can be little doubt that our sexual revolution has not really uprooted the weed of the flesh.

The devil, as we have said, works through the world and the flesh to accomplish his ends. When we say the third weed of scripture is the devil himself, what then do we add to the preceding? We suggested that his working on the heart and soul of men and women — through religious phenomena, in interior prayer, etc., — is the "third force," the third weed in the Lord's harvest field. Sometimes, as C.S. Lewis observes, the devil has his greatest success in convincing us that he does not exist. This can be especially effective in the type of secularized, naturalistic culture we have described above. At other times, he can present distorted ideas of himself and his power (and thus of God and his power) which lead to fear and superstition and block any genuine encounter with the Good Shepherd of the gospels. This may be more common in more "primitive" societies, but when you see a movie like *The Exorcist* you wonder. What idea of the supernatural, and of God and Satan, would such a portrayal convey to the viewers? They might be terrified or they might consider the whole story fantastic and foolish, but it is difficult to conceive how such a portrayal of satanic power could bring them any closer to true discernment.

While much more could be said about the three weeds today, these brief reflections may make clear that all three are alive and flourishing. Which are most abundant in your own life — this was the second part of the question — only you can say. But it is important that you *can* say. The one weed which has no value and can kill the whole harvest is self-delusion, the unwillingness to know and face our real situation before the Lord. On the other hand, the more we grow in discerning love, the more we know ourselves. And then the Lord of the harvest will turn the remaining weeds to good.

Chapter 9: Discerning Love and Humility

Our final practicum question asks about the relationship between the habit of discerning love and St. Ignatius' famous third degree (or kind) of humility. The latter has often been called the high point of Ignatius' whole mysticism of service. It is, however, difficult for most retreatants to accept since it appears to require that we pray for humiliations, insults and poverty, something which most sincere pray-ers find very difficult to do. After years of directing retreats and of facing the challenge of the third degree in my own retreats, however, I am convinced that this is not really what Ignatius intended. To desire insults and reproaches does smack of masochism; moreover, it is difficult to see how such a desire would be the culminating point in the whole process of the *Spiritual Exercises*.

The *Exercises* are intended as a means to free the generous soul from all disordered attachments, in order that she may find and follow the will of God for her. After the "first week" of the 30-day retreat, the soul should, as it were, be naked before the Lord: Her masks should be removed and she should be able to stand before him in radical honesty and humility. The "second week," which is the heart of the *Exercises*, is then the time to be filled with Christ, to put on the Lord Jesus, to allow myself to be refashioned in his image, so that his values and attitudes become my own. It is at the end of this second week that Ignatius proposes the culminating meditation on the three degrees of humility, of which the third degree is the climax. It presents the ideal for the soul desirous of living totally "in, with, and for Christ."

If we look at the text again (as quoted in the practicum question) in the light of this explanation of the dynamics of the *Spiritual Exercises*, I think it is clear that the important words are "like Christ . . . with Christ . . . for Christ." I do not desire poverty and insults for their own sake, nor even as an ascetical ideal. Jesus himself did not do this, as his prayer in the Garden of Gethsemane makes clear. Rather, he desired to be totally one with the Father, *whatever* the cost, and wherever it might lead him. In the third degree, we desire the same: to be with Jesus, to be one with him wherever he goes. The "Wherever you go, I shall go" of the first chapter of the Book of Ruth is, I think, a beautiful expression of the third degree of humility. Ruth did not wish to be an alien in an alien land, a widow forever, but she did desire to live her whole life with Naomi, her mother-in-law, whatever this might entail.

This is the third degree of humility to which the *Spiritual Exercises* lead us. The connection to our discussion of the habit of discerning love is perhaps clear already. One who possesses this habitual sensitivity to the Lord is one who has lived long in his love, and for whom he has become the absolute center and whole meaning of life. For such a one, all that matters is to be with Christ — in poverty, insults, success, glory, whatever. The how is much less important than the what.

This is indeed great love, and one who possesses it will be the perfect apostle. We cannot achieve it; we made this clear in discussing the habit of discerning love, and Ignatius makes it clear in telling us that we can only "desire to be chosen" for the third degree of humility. It is pure gift — God's gift. But as I always tell my retreatants, don't ask for it unless you really desire it. The Lord is dying — has died — to give it to us. Thus if we also sincerely desire it, he will surely give us this most perfect of his gifts.